About the Prophets

By Harry N. Huxhold

Fairway Press
Lima, Ohio

ABOUT THE PROPHETS

FIRST EDITION
Copyright © 1990 by
Harry N. Huxhold

7724 / ISBN 1-55673-263-5 PRINTED IN U.S.A.

To
Richard Pioch
who encouraged the study
which resulted in this modest work
and
to
Angeline and Henry J. Meyers
who made its publication
possible

Contents

A Preface

In the *Twelve Who Followed* (Augsburg, 1987), I referred to Edgar J. Goodspeed's observation that our information about the Twelve Apostles is so scanty that one would be hard pressed to fill out an obituary notice for most of them. The same is true, if not even more so, for the prophets. Consequently, we are all the more curious about them.

After the publication of the *Twelve Who Followed*, our Sunday adult Bible class pressed their curiosity about the prophets. They requested that we study together what we could about the prophetic figures.

This little book about the prophets is the result. This study is a careful effort to research what we can learn about the prophets as persons. The futility of the effort to offer more biographical data than the scanty materials made available is not meaningless. We have to be impressed with the fact that the prophetic witness is greater than the prophet.

It is an outstanding tribute to the prophets that their roles as the spokesmen for God were preserved with the emphasis on the word they have received from God. The diversity of the manner in which they were called should not be ignored. Nor should one overlook their private struggles with the God who called them.

What follows is an attempt to help the readers put into perspective the message of the prophets. While what we may know about the prophets may remain vague, their message should not. We should remember them for what they said. That is how they would like to be remembered.

What should be most striking about the prophets is not that they were always harsh and strident voices thundering judgment. At the heart of their message was always the call for people to remember the grace God had revealed in the covenant God had made with his people. That is how God would like you to remember the prophets.

Harry N. Huxhold

The Prophetic Office

When we approach the subject of the prophets, we are helped in our study by noting a differentiation between the prophets that is built into the Hebrew Bible. The Hebrew Scriptures are divided into three parts — Law, Prophets and Writings. The Law, or Torah, is the Pentateuch or Five Books of Moses. The Prophets are divided into the Former Prophets and the Latter Prophets. The four books listed in our English Bible as Joshua, Judges, 1 and 2 Samuel, and 1 and 2 Kings are the Former Prophets. The Latter Prophets are Isaiah, Jeremiah, Ezekiel and the Twelve. The Twelve, which constitute one volume, are the prophets we refer to as the Minor Prophets. Lamentations and Daniel are listed among the Writings which are Psalms, Job, Proverbs, Ruth, Song of Songs, Ecclesiastes, Lamentations, Esther, Daniel, Ezra, Nehemiah and 1 and 2 Chronicles.

The subject of prophecy is an intriguing one. Much of the popular fascination with prophecy is the regard for prophecy as the art of predicting the future. Such a limited approach to the writings of the prophets is to rummage through their materials for clues as to how the present can be identified with what prophets predicted and to use the prophets as models for foretelling the future. While it is true that the prophets have insights to the future of God's rule, they were not involved in simple prediction. Furthermore, such a narrow view of the prophetic task is to rob the message of the prophet who addressed urgent social and political issues in the light of God's rule.

Moses as Model

The office of the prophet was established early in the life of God's people. Moses, the leader and mediator for the Children of Israel, was a model for the prophetic office to be continued as an assurance to the people of God's gracious presence and direction for them. In the Book of Deuteronomy, Moses delivered his farewell address to the people in the form of a second giving of the Law. The promise of God to Moses is also stated, "I will raise up for them a prophet like you from among their brethren; and I will put my words in his mouth, and he shall speak to them all that I command him." (Deuteronomy 18:18) The people were ready to obey the word of the prophet which God would authenticate.

The stories of how God worked for the people through the prophets is well rehearsed through the stories of the Former Prophets. In the narratives of Judges, Samuel and Kings, prophets appear to give the prophetic office its continuity. Samuel, who stands tallest among them as a national leader, fits into the picture with Nathan, Gad, Shemiah, Ahijah and Jehu ben Hanani. The acts of Elijah and Elisha are recorded in 1 and 2 Kings. These accounts record how faithful and heroic the prophets were.

Prophetic Collections

The nature of the books we call the Latter Prophets took an entirely different turn with the collection of materials that reflect the nature of the work of the prophets in the eighth, seventh and early sixth centuries, B.C. We know these materials to be the classical literature of the Golden Age of Prophecy. These books are comprised largely of sermons, oracles, poems and sayings the prophets uttered on special occasions. Sometimes these materials contain messages identified with unknown prophets. The books associated with this period are Amos, Hosea, Isaiah, Micah, Zephaniah, Nahum, Habakkuk and Jeremiah.

The Silver Age of Prophecy is identified as the late sixth and early fifth centuries when Haggai and Zechariah carried on their ministries. Ezekiel and the second half of Isaiah are also identified as exilic prophets and Obadiah, Joel and Malachi are also placed into the post-exilic period.

Daniel and Jonah are exceptional to the regular books of the prophets since they are narratives about prophets and are not the collections of materials found in the other books of those we call the "writing prophets."

Prophets and Priests

The prophetic office that began with Moses was identified strongly with the priestly office from its earliest stages. Moses himself was of the Tribe of Levi, the tribe dedicated to the priesthood. (Exodus 2:1-2) Moses' brother Aaron was linked with Moses' prophetic task (Exodus 4:13-17) and his sister Miriam was regarded as a prophetess. (Exodus 16:20) The prophet Samuel was a protege of the priest Eli at the temple. (1 Samuel 3) Elijah played the role of the priest in building an altar and offering prayers and oblation. (1 Kings 18:30-39) Jeremiah was one of the priests of Anathoth, (Jeremiah 1:1) and Ezekiel is identified as a priest. (Ezekiel 1:3) Isaiah, who may have been a priest, received a stirring vision and call to the prophetic office at the temple. (Isaiah 6)

Priestly Equipment

That the priestly office was linked to the prophetic task was symbolized by the pouch which the priest wore as a "breastpiece of judgment," (Exodus 28:15) which contained the sacred lots *Urim* and *Thummim* (Exodus 28:30) which were used by the priest to get an oracular decision. (Leviticus 8:8, Numbers 27:21, Deuteronomy 33:8, 1 Samuel 14:4-42 and 23:6-13)

In Hebrew the prophets were known as the *nabi*. The origin of that word is questionable, but it came to mean the equivalent of our "announcer." The prophet was one who announced the word which came from God. The word also designated one who was influenced and controlled by the spirit. In some instances this was an ecstatic experience (1 Samuel 19:20-24) and was possible in alien situations. (Numbers 22:24)

Prophetic Guilds

In its most primitive stages the prophetic office was indistinguishable from the work of the seers, who had the gift of interpreting the signs of the day. (1 Samuel 9:9) In time prophetic schools and guilds developed. Some obviously were only for the sake of a livelihood (2 Kings 6:1-2, 2:3, 3:11, 4:1) and others may have been ascetic. (Amos 2:11, 1 Chronicles 2:55, Jeremiah 35:5)

Because there were various people who laid claim to being prophets it was necessary to distinguish between those who brought the authentic word from God and those who brought promise of a hollow peace. (Jeremiah 6:14) The manner in which the people were to sort out the false from the true prophetic word was whether the "word does not come to pass or come true." (Deuteronomy 18:22) The manner in which the great prophets did deliver this word was their interpretation of their times and future in the light of the Exodus event and the Covenant.

Fulfillment

Jesus stepped into the succession of the prophets as one who not only maintained the tradition of the prophets, but as the One who was the fulfillment of all that the prophets had revealed. Jesus did not come only to fulfill the messianic office as prophets before him had envisioned it, but he was present in the very promises they had made. The messages, the styles, the approaches, the sympathies, the empathies, the hopes of the whole entourage of the prophets came to their fulfillment in Jesus of Nazareth. The writer to the Hebrews said it well, "In many and various ways God spoke of old to our fathers by the prophets; but in these last days he has spoken to us by a Son. (Hebrews 1:1)

Jesus himself bemoaned the fact that the prophets as a lot had suffered persecution and martyrdom. Jesus knew he would suffer the same fate in spite of the fact that he would have gladly offered Jerusalem eternal security like a mother hen gathers her brood. (Matthew 24:29-39) The same rhythm of salvation which God worked out through the long succession of prophets sent to proclaim a message of redemption God worked out in the life, death and resurrection of Jesus Christ. All the prophetic office is of one piece and applicable today for those who listen to the prophetic word:

> *You are built upon the foundation of the apostles and prophets, Christ Jesus himself, being the cornerstone, in whom the whole structure is joined together and grows into a holy temple in the Lord; in whom you also are build into it for a dwelling place of God in the Spirit.*
> Ephesians 2:19-22

1. Amos

THE SHEPHERD OF TEKOA

Amos was one of those strange but exciting people who had the remarkable sensitivities that suited him to be a prophetic voice among the people of God. He was identified as one who was "among the shepherds of Tekoa (1:1)." Tekoa was a town about six miles south of Bethlehem. The wilderness of that area where he tended his sheep was a desolate rocky area surrounded by limestone hills. Typically it was a place where this thoughtful shepherd could meditate on the plight of his people and concern himself with the manner in which God had revealed himself in their history.

When Amos journeyed into the Northern Kingdom, where later he established his ministry, he discovered reasons to worry for his people. At that moment (750 B.C.) in the eighth century B.C. the people were enjoying some tranquility and prosperity. Assyria was the dominant power, but it had withdrawn from Israel, and the economy was on the upswing because of the success of the trade routes. Amos knew this interlude of prosperity had to be short-lived. The people surmised that their successes were linked to the favoritism they enjoyed as the people of God. They did not worry about the threat that the world super powers were to them. They wanted to make the most of that glorious moment and lived in the ecstasy of their unrealistic optimism.

Signs of the Times

Amos assessed their situation differently. As a shepherd he had seen a plague of locusts devastate the land. He surmised that if God could wipe out crops with a hoard of locusts, what could he do if he sent his judgment upon the people? He looked out on the burning drought that consumed the farmlands, and he wondered what would happen if God would unleash the burning fires of his judgment upon his people. He saw other evidences of God's judgment in nature as compelling reasons why he should carry the words of prophetic warning to the people. (7:1-6) If the people thought that their rebounding economy had been the result of their religiosity and their piety, he saw things quite differently. What was going on in the economy was not the result of some divine blessings. The economy was booming for some because of the greedy manipulations of enterprising people. (4:1-3)

Not all were being blessed. The rich were getting richer, and the poor were getting poorer. Amos was able to see that the comforts of wealth had blinded them to the needs of the poor. He sensed that the enthusiasm of the new rich for the possibilities they saw in the economy made them indifferent to the threats to the welfare of the nation. Above all, Amos was convinced that God could not tolerate this blatant disregard of what God expected of his people for his word. The people simply could not go against God's will and expect that he would not bring down his judgment upon them. Unless the people woke up and repented of their sins, they were doomed. Their social sin was their preoccupation with wealth.

Greedynomics

Certainly Amos would never have questioned the advantage of a booming economy if there were not problems with it. God had promised special blessings to people for their faithful industry. The Hebrews did have a good work ethic. There is obviously blessing for those who are diligent in their vocations. However, Amos was deeply disturbed by what he witnessed in the market place in the conduct of some business people. Amos discerned that the profit motives of some made them totally indifferent to the needs of the poor. In fact, some of these people even contributed to the plight of the poor. They took advantage of every opportunity, and in doing so, they took advantage of people (8:4-6)

These people were so greedy and hungry for profits that they could hardly wait for the bell to ring to start their trading. They grew restless on the sabbath, and they could not wait for the holy days to end so that they could get back to their desks and their counters. The sabbath and the holy days, of course, were meant to be times when people could rest from their labors and contemplate the goodness of God. But the whole time these people had to lay down their briefcases, set aside their money bags, and their tools of trade, they were thinking of new business deals and how they could improve their financial picture. They thought of every way they could to inflate their money, cheat on the measures and use false balances to give the people short weights on what they ordered. The people who suffered, of course, were the poor.

God's Unhappiness

Amos was not the only one who witnessed what was going on among these shrewd business people. God also saw through their schemes. Amos says, "The Lord had sworn by the pride of Jacob: 'Surely I will never forget any of their deeds.' " (8:7) Moses had appealed to God for the salvation of Israel on the basis of the promises God had made to his people. Here Amos indicates that the same promises are the reason that God will not forget the poor and those who are abused by the rich and powerful. If the prosperity in the land had lulled the people into thinking that God was pleased with Israel, they had another guess coming. If they had increased their contributions to the temple that would not assume that they could thereby buy the favors of God. God would not forget their sins against his children, the creatures whom he had fashioned out of love.

15

Amos did not suggest that the poor were the favorites of God. God does not favor them over the rich. However, because the poor are so neglected and despised, God must give special attention to them, because no one else wants to. It is therefore a common theme running through the Hebrew Scriptures that God will not forget the *ha aretz,* the poor people. It is a special sign of God's loving care and concern for all the world that he does care about those for whom no one cares. The message of Amos stands. Any society in which the poor get poorer, because the rich get richer, stands under the judgment of God.

No Social Security

The prophet Amos preached against the people as he did because of the manner in which they went about trying to insure their future. They were trying to guarantee their social security at a great price. There were times of unparalleled wealth in the Northern Kingdom under Jeroboam II. This was the third great wave of prosperity, because at this moment the people were controlling the trade routes during an interval of sustained peace. For this the people felt they were being especially blessed by God.

It was the smugness about their prosperity that Amos attacked. "Woe to those who are at ease in Zion, and to those who feel secure on the mountain of Samaria." (6:1) These people had not found their security in the God who gave them blessings. They found their security in the things they thought came from God. They had passed that line of contentment and exaggerated their need for more things. Amos cites what they were. Their extravagance extended to fancy beds made from ivory. They ate the finest choices of meat. The excesses included drinking wine from bowls rather than from just goblets and cups, and they covered themselves with the finest oils and perfumes. (6:4-6)

What was so dreadful about those people who had become rich in Amos' day was that they thought they were better than other people. With great sarcasm the prophet calls them "the notable men" (6:1) who believed that everyone should come to them for advice. But he asked them to go and take a look at other cities. He wants to know if the noble men can actually boast that they are better "than these kingdoms." What would make them think they were so much better? Amos denounced this pride that the people attached to their wealth.

Putting off the Evil Day

Yet Amos would not be critical of such people on the grounds alone that they were prideful and showy. Their real problem was that they "put far away the evil day." They simply did not want to face the day of reckoning. They did not feel accountable for what was happening to them and around them. They were unwilling to be realistic about how fragile their wealth was. They were sitting upon the "seat of violence" and destruction and did not know it. They were making money as fast as they could while the trade routes held open. They were unrealistic about the super power Assyria that could crush them at will. (6:2-3)

Amos also knew that the very fact that these people in the Northern Kingdom were flaunting their riches so much made them a prime target for a takeover by a superpower. Worse than that, these people did not demonstrate that they felt a sense of accountability to the God of history who controlled the nations. If only these people would repent and turn to God instead of their riches they could forestall this kind of judgment. Instead, God would use their enemies against them and destroy them. Amos foretells that, because they are unrepentant, "they will be the first to go into exile." (6:7)

The sign of their unrepentant attitude is that "they are not grieved over the ruin of Joseph." These are the kind of people who only thought of themselves when they were amassing their wealth, and when they lose it all, they will not grieve for the others of their nation who lost everything, and the loss of the people as such. They only grieve for themselves and what they lost. They only worried for themselves to begin with, and that is why they will go into exile. They had no sympathy for the poor while they were enriching themselves, how could they have sympathy for anyone else but themselves? That finally was their chief sin.

Amos saw no hope for the Northern Kingdom. He completed his preaching about 750 B.C., and within the generation (721 B.C.) the Assyrians carried the citizens of Samaria into captivity. So striking is the message of Amos about the hopeless state of Israel's unbelief that some scholars believe the message of restoration (9:9-15) comes from a later scribe.

2. Hosea

THE FAITHFUL HUSBAND

Hosea, the son of Beeri, is unique among the Hebrew prophets since he is the only one of the writing prophets who had his hometown in the Northern Kingdom of Israel. Elijah had left a great prophetic tradition in the Northern Kingdom, but that was forgotten by the time of Hosea. Amos had finished his ministry only a few years earlier. When he began his work about 745 B.C., Hosea found things so bad that he accused prophets and priests alike of the neglect of their offices, of fostering pagan practices and not knowing the true God of Israel. While he preached vigorously against these sins and the sins of the people, no other prophet of the Old Testament delivers a message of God's love for his people more eloquently than Hosea.

The prophet saw in his own marriage a parable of God's love for his bride, the Church, which was then Israel. Married to a harlot named Gomer, who left him only to be sold into slavery, Hosea went and purchased her in the slave market to make her his honorable wife and to be faithful husband to her. For Hosea this relationship to his unfaithful wife and his redeeming love for her signaled what God had to endure in his love for Israel. As Hosea out of love had to go to the market place to rescue his wife from her self-imposed doom, so God must out of grace and love interrupt the life of slavery to sin and death that this adulterous nation had brought upon itself. (Chapters 1, 3) Hosea names the children born to him and Gomer: Jezreel, Not Pitied and Not My People, to signal the tragic relationship that existed between God and Israel.

Pain for God

Israel did not make it easy for God. Specifically, the prophet could announce one sin atop another as the occasions for God's frustrations with Israel. (Chapters 7-10) Hosea spoke out against the alliances which Israel was trying to establish in order to protect himself. The king of Israel had made an alliance against the Assyrians. When the king of the Southern Kingdom, the kingdom of Judea, refused to join the allegiance, Israel invaded the Southern Kingdom. However, that only drew fire from the Assyrians who invaded the northern districts of Israel. This was the beginning of the end. Only a few years later Assyria would utterly destroy the Northern Kingdom and the ten tribes of Israel would be taken into captivity.

Remarkably the sermons, oracles and pronouncements of the prophet Hosea were preserved in the Southern Kingdom of Judah as a reminder of how God had to deal with his people in the Northern Kingdom. What is noteworthy, though, is that the total appeal of the work of the prophet to this nation which appeared doomed comes out of the great heart of God's love and the ardent appeal to still win back this straying and decadent nation. God, the husband, who is sickened by the behavior of his adulterous wife, Israel, still remembers the Exodus as an idyllic honeymoon, and has an ardent a love as the day he first made his marital covenant with his bride, Israel. (11:1-4) Out of that deep love God made an appeal for repentance. "I will return again to my place, until they acknowledge their guilt and seek my face, and in their distress they seek me." (5:15)

What Israel had failed to see was that God was the One to whom she should have returned in all her difficulties. She should have known that God had made her weak when she thought she was strong. He was the One who had laid a heavy hand upon her. She was in a weakened, sickly condition because of all her sins and her unfaithfulness. But when she saw her sickness and her frailty, she had returned to the Assyrians.

But God had said, "the great king (of Assyria) is not able to cure you or heal your wound." (5:13) For that reason God even plotted further against Israel. God threatened to be like a lion against Israel, to lie in wait for the kill, to carry Israel off without anyone being able to rescue her. (5:13-14) God would wait for Israel to say, "Come, let us return to the Lord; for he has torn, that he may heal us; he has stricken, and he will bind us up. After two days he will revive us; on the third day he will raise us up, that we may live before him." (6:1-2) God was willing to accept this people once again, but the people had to know that it was God who was in charge all the while. It was God who was pushing the people toward himself, if only they would come.

God Looks for Love

The prophet made clear what God was looking for, "I desire steadfast love and not sacrifice, the knowledge of God, rather than burnt offerings." (6:6) Hosea witnessed the confused religious picture of the day. It was not as though the people were not religious. They were that indeed. The people did have a state religion. This was in the latter half of the eighth century before Christ in the Northern Kingdom. Worship of the god Baal, the great fertility god of Canaan, had been forbidden. There was no want of religious practice.

The people performed rituals and sacrifices. They were devoted to offering what was required of them at their shrines. Yet all of this was perfunctory and mechanistic. In reality the people were still worshiping Baal. They simply had taken over the language of the liturgical sacrifices to cover their actual worship of Baal in the hopes that he would give them fertile land, bless their crops and usher in prosperity. All the signs of orthodoxy, conservatism and diligent pietism were there, but the signs were only a cover for the faithlessness of the people.

Better than Sacrifice

In dealing with this people God worked out of his *chesed*, his steadfast love, faithfulness and grace. For this reason God required that people respond to him also out of steadfast love rather than out of sacrifice. That sounds strange when we realize that the Hebrew Scriptures prescribe that the people should bring their sacrifices. However, here God was saying that any sacrifice that is meant to be manipulative of God is a denial of the relationship which God wants to exist between God and people. People do not make sacrifices in order to create a relationship with God. The relationship already exists because of God's steadfast love for his people.

Similarly God states his preference, "The knowledge of God rather than burnt offerings." (6:6) Here again, this would appear somewhat mystical when the liturgical laws of Israel definitely called for burnt offerings. God does not want the burnt offerings to jeopardize that God had revealed what is meant to be godly. God had made abundantly clear the intention to be a gracious God who called this people to be a part of the kingly and godly rule.

Hosea's message of God's faithful and unswerving love for Israel as the love of a faithful husband epitomizes the message of grace throughout the prophets. Jesus' use of the same relationship to depict his love for the church is recorded several times throughout the Gospels, and the Pauline application of this intimacy is well known. (Ephesians 5:22-32)

3. Isaiah

THE PROPHET OF RIGHTEOUSNESS

The occasion for the call of Isaiah as a prophet (6:1-13) is spectacular. The circumstances are extraordinary. This account is one of the best known and most frequently quoted portions of Scripture to explain the relationship of God and his prophets or servants. It is regarded by most biblical scholars to be a vivid account of an authentic personal experience. It is most helpful in describing the making of a prophet. The time is mentioned as "In the year that King Uzziah died." The year was approximately 742 B.C. The fact that it was in the year that Uzziah dies does not mean that Uzziah had already died. The phrase suggests quite strongly that the occasion for the vision of Isaiah was some festival, such as New Year's Day, when the cultic ceremonies honored the divine king being enthroned as the conqueror and victor over all the enemies of his people. At the high point of such a ceremony the excitement and color of the rituals may have produced the ripe moment for the ecstatic vision of Isaiah. The scene is set at the temple.

The content of the vision is overpowering. What Isaiah sees is the train of the garment of the Lord as he sits upon a throne. Even that glimpse of glory is so dramatic as to fill the temple with the awesomeness of God's presence. The building shakes, and the place is filled with smoke. While Isaiah does not see God himself, he does see the seraphim. The seraphim are angels attendant to the throne of God. Their name means "burning ones." They are the ones who burn things as when one brings the burning coal. They also appear to have the faces, hands and voices of men and are capable of standing upright. The seraphim had six wings. Two were used to cover the face in the presence of God's glory, two to cover their nakedness and two were used for flying. They sang antiphonally to each other. We are not sure there were only two. However many angels, the scene must have been splendid and overpowering.

He is Overcome

However, the scene was so awesome as to make Isaiah extremely uncomfortable. He is overcome by a sense of unworthiness. Not only does he become entranced by the beauty of the scene, but he senses the holiness of the moment. The song of the seraphim, "Holy, holy, holy is the Lord of hosts; the whole earth is full of his glory," not only resounds in the temple but reverberates in his heart and mind. He confesses with fear and trembling, "Woe is me! For I am lost; for I am a man of unclean lips, and I dwell in the midst of a people of unclean lips; for my eyes have seen the King, the Lord of hosts!" The song of the seraphim which sounded the trisagion, the three holies, is reflected most strongly in the writings of Isaiah. As a prophet he never lost sight of the holiness.

The unworthiness that Isaiah felt at the instance was overpowered by the action of one of the seraphim. The seraph flies to Isaiah with a burning coal which he had taken from the altar with tongs and touches the mouth of Isaiah. The seraph then speaks the word of absolution to Isaiah, "Behold, this has touched your lips; your guilt is taken away, and your sin forgiven." The unworthy one is made worthy. The sinful one has been made righteous. The unclean one has been cleansed. The one who could not speak on behalf of God has now been readied for that high calling. The ecstatic experience of the holy has now become a reality that can be turned into action.

He Responds

The response to this act of purification was almost immediate. Isaiah hears the voice of the Lord saying, "Whom shall I send, and who will go for us?'' Then Isaiah said, ''Here am I! Send me!'' Whatever weaknesses or inadequacies Isaiah had felt otherwise were not noticeable to him now. All was covered by this experience of God's grace. Isaiah was prepared and made adequate by the embrace of God's love in the forgiveness of sins. So profound was the experience of God's mercy that Isaiah volunteers to go forth on behalf of God when God debates over the question of who should go on his behalf.

All Isaiah is supposed to do is get out there and give the word, but the more that he does, the more some people might refuse to believe. That does raise some misgivings in the heart and mind of Isaiah. Here he was all primed to go out and tell everyone how wonderful and gracious, loving and forgiving his God is, and nobody is supposed to be able to understand him. Isaiah asks, ''How long, O Lord?'' That was a fair question. How long was he expected to go out and tell the good news about God only to get the bad news about the results.

The answer that came back does not appear to be very comforting. God responds that Isaiah should go on with his work until cities lie waste and the land is desolate and there are many forsaken places.

How Long?

As it was, the superscription of the book (1:1) tells us Isaiah ministered during the reign of four kings of Judah. They were Uzziah, Jotham, Ahaz and Hezekiah. This would be a period extending from 742 to approximately 700 B.C. The beginning years of Isaiah's ministry were occupied with concerns for the social conditions in Judah. (Chapters 1-5) At the same time Judah had to be alert to the threat of the approaching Assyrian armies.

When Ahaz was king, he refused to listen to the prophet, (7:12) and it appears that Isaiah retreated from public life for a time (8:11-22) until the occasion of Ahaz's death when (14:28) he felt called upon to prophesy again. Some of the well known oracles (9:2-7, 11, 9) which the Christian Church identifies as messianic came from this period.

A Change

Isaiah turned his attention from the social sins of his own people to the divine will and purpose for the larger scene. The prophet speaks oracles against Babylon, (13:1-22) Moab (15:1—16:3) and Damascus. (17:1-3) At the same time he calls his people back to the faith in the God who rules over all (17:4-14) and God's people would survive under God's care, compassion (14:1-4) and God's ultimate purpose (14:24-27).

The prophet suggests that the reason Israel can take heart in the face of doom is because they can trust God. God says, "Come, my people, enter your chambers, and shut your doors behind you; hide yourself for a little while until the wrath is past." (26:20). Another reason that Israel can take comfort is that God's judgment is worked out upon the world. They can run to God for solace and comfort and hide in the warmth of his love and be assured that he will work out justice upon the world. "For behold the Lord is coming forth out of his place to punish the inhabitants of the earth for their iniquity." (26:21) All of history testifies to that fact. The cruel ones and the oppressors rise up only to be cut down eventually. (31:4, 5)

Take Heart

The prophet promises that God destroys the sea monster Leviathan, the twisting and fleeing serpent, the dragon of chaos, who has been keeping everything in turmoil since the beginning of creation. (27:1) This is the final overthrow of the enemies of God and consequently, the destruction of the worst enemies. God ultimately wipes out the evil one. That, we of course, see accomplished in the life and death of our Lord when the Lord Jesus himself knows that the "Prince of this world is judged." (John 12:31)

Israel can be stouthearted and confident in the face of all adversity. The prophet says, "Thou dost keep him in perfect peace, whose mind is stayed on thee, because he trusts in thee. Trust in the Lord forever, for the Lord God is an everlasting rock." (26:3, 4) Israel had trusted the wrong gods. The prophet confesses for them, "O Lord our God, other lords besides thee have ruled over us, but thy name alone we acknowledge." (26:13)

God Saves

No human accomplishments can match what God has done. God's name is remembered for those great and mighty acts which endure forever. They endure not only because they saved the people for the moment or because God saved the day for them, but because the great and mighty acts of God were assurances that God could also save and deliver them from death itself. The prophet can burst with rousing song, "The dead shall live, their bodies shall rise. O dwellers in the dust, awake and sing for joy! For thy dew is a dew of light, and on the land of the shades thou wilt let it fall." (26:19)

Isaiah concluded his long ministry in the high confidence that one could rely upon the promises of God for deliverance from the judgment that came upon the people. In 701 Hezekiah would pay tribute to Sennacherib to save Jerusalem for that moment, and God saved Jerusalem from the hand of Sennacherib when "the angel of the Lord went forth and slew a hundred and eighty five thousand in the camp of the Assyrians." (37:36) Isaiah knew the worst was yet to come, (39:5) but his steadfast prayer was what he had preached so faithfully, "My soul yearns for thee in the night, my spirit within me earnestly seeks thee." (26:9)

Isaiah envisioned the eschatological day when God would "swallow up death forever." (25:8) He pictured this in terms of his own day when Gould would set things right for his own people and would settle peace on the nations. That day did not

27

arrive in Isaiah's time and it was not until the Day of our Lord's Resurrection many centuries later that the day did see its fulfillment. Yet, Isaiah knew that not only was God capable of dealing with death in this manner and that ultimately he would, but that it was the very nature of God to do so. Isaiah believed that God is the Lord of Life and Death. "It will be said on that day, 'Lo, this is our God' and we have waited for him, that he might save us. This is the Lord; we have waited for him; let us be glad and rejoice in his salvation." (25:9)

4. Micah

THE RURAL PROPHET

Micah, a younger contemporary of Isaiah, was anything but a minor prophet as we like to call the Twelve. He ranked with the great prophets of the eighth century before Christ. He is credited with having induced a period of repentance among the people in a time of crisis. His followers believed that he was responsible for the sparing of Jerusalem. He was also cited as one who had a great deal of influence upon King Hezekiah, who instituted many reforms that were favorable for the prosperity of Jerusalem. It is rather striking that the social prophet, who preached the vigorous sermons in the first part of his book, (Chapters 1, 2, 3, 6) should offer the hope of reconstruction. (7:8-20)

It was, of course, typical of the prophets, who could forewarn of judgment and doom to call their people to repentance, that they would also remind the people that their God Jahweh would never renege on the promises he had given to their fathers. God in his faithfulness would also send a ruler to set things right for his people. (5:2-4) The kind of ruler whom God would send would be in the best of their tradition. That tradition was exemplified by the ruler whom God had sent once before, David, the son of Jesse, who had been born in the rural town of Bethlehem.

God Could Repent

God had sent his people a great ruler from that town once before, and he could do it again. Micah makes it clear. He is talking about Bethlehem in the region of Ephrathath. This Bethlehem is not to be confused with any other Bethlehem like the one in the region of Zebulon. This is that little hick town six miles south west of Jerusalem, maybe five miles the way the crow flies. This town surely was "little to be among the clans of Judah." Towns ordinarily had to be about one thousand inhabitants to qualify to be on the map. This one did not make that grade.

However, Micah believed that the town had already established its reputation as being a town of great distinction. The town could boast of the fact that one of its sons had made it big as king. It was no small matter to brag about the fact that the Warrior King David had come from this region. The career of David was known well enough. David had slain the giant Goliath when David was still a mere sapling. That was only the beginning of his accomplishments. He had brought together the northern and southern tribes and welded them together into one kingdom. He had extended the borders of Israel. He had conquered all of Israel's enemies. He brought fame and respectability to Israel as a nation. He had founded a monarchy that was to last some five hundred years. Already at the time of Micah the monarchy to Judah had survived for about three hundred years. Thus when Micah thinks of Bethlehem as producing one more favorite son to rule, he says "from you shall come forth for me one who is to be ruler in Israel, whose origin is from old, from ancient days." (5:2)

Comfort in Continuity

There was something very comforting about this kind of continuity. The ruler who is to come has his roots in this hometown of the great heroic king David. It was as though God was going to give it another shot. Micah knew that the monarchy which had survived many trials and tribulations through three centuries would be put under greater tests and would ultimately collapse. However, God would not be left without a plan. He would start all over and create a kingdom that would endure. Yet it was all of one piece. That God who had started with David had never given up. He had stayed with his people through thick and thin, and he would begin again.

Micah came from a rural area and lived in one of those smaller towns that lined a trade route. That was his vantage point for observing national and international events. He knew that Samaria, the capital of Israel in the north, was doomed. However, he had also to warn his fellow countrymen in the Southern Kingdom that Jerusalem, their capital, could and would also fall. (3:9-12) Judah was already a weak vassal state, and Hezekiah persisted in anti-Assyrian policies. He sounded the warning, "Therefore he shall give them up until the time when she who is in travail has brought forth." (5:3)

A New King

Micah pictures the time when Judah would go into exile. He envisions this like a time of travail when a mother is giving birth to a child. So Israel is to have travail and pain, but then like a mother she is to give birth to a new king who would bring restoration to his people and who would make things right for God's people. "Then the rest of his brethren shall return to the people of Israel." (5:3) God would raise up this new king who would rule in the style of the King David. What the prophet held out to his people here was to form a messianic hope and dream for years to come. It is this dream that evangelists and apostles saw fulfilled in the coming of Jesus, born in Bethlehem.

However, even before the evangelists related this prophetic oracle to the birth of Jesus, there undoubtedly was a strong messianic tradition that the messiah would be born in Bethlehem. That tradition was based on this oracle. There was a strong desire to believe that the messiah would be a second David. The complaint that Jesus came from Nazareth was because the people did not know he was born in Bethlehem and

31

their expectation was that the Messiah should be. Also, Matthew recorded that when the magi came in search of the king the palace scribes sent them to Bethlehem on the basis of this oracle.

The Second Coming

The early Christian community recognized that it was Jesus who so aptly fit the description of the prophetic oracle. No post exilic king came to fit the bill. It was by faith that the church early on recognized that the davidic kingdom so richly promised to ancient Israel is none other than the rule of Jesus who rules us by his grace and love. That is the thrust of this message about the ruler who comes from Bethlehem. Like David before him, he will be a faithful shepherd. "He shall stand and feed his flock in the strength of the Lord." (5:4) David had come off the fields of Bethlehem where he had tended sheep to rule the people of God. The messianic king who comes will rule the people of God like a careful and tender-hearted shepherd who is willing to give his life for his sheep.

The blessings that accrue to his people, because God sends this ruler of grace and love at Bethlehem, is that the people of God shall dwell secure. The prophet writes, "And they shall dwell secure, for now he shall be great to the ends of the earth." (5:4) Real security lies in what this ruler does. He has defeated the worst enemies: sin, death and hell. Where the prophecy from Micah which names Bethlehem as the birthplace of the Messiah is read in Adventtide, the word means much more than that the prophet predicted it. The word is the assurance that God was working out the plan of redemption consistent with the manner in which God had operated out of grace in the past.

5. Zephaniah

THE DOOMSDAY PROPHET

The prophet Zephaniah was of royal descent. The superscription of his book (1:1) indicates that one of his ancestors was Hezekiah, the renown Judean king (715-687 B.C.), who was served by the prophets Isaiah and Micah. Zephaniah was a second cousin once removed from King Josiah (640-609). The prophet may have ministered about 630-625 B.C., sometime before the reforms of King Josiah in 621 B.C. (2 Kings 23)

A shorter book, the message of the prophet is divided easily into three chapters which separate the subject matter. The first chapter speaks judgment upon Judah because of Judah's corrupt and perverted religious practices and syncretistic worship. Chapter two inveys against other nations, particularly those who are the enemies of Judah, because of their idolatries and their persecution of God's people. Chapter three is filled with comfort for Judah after their repentance, following upon the catastrophe and the renewal of God's love. It is obvious from the definite shifts from the first into the third person in these materials that a disciple of Zephaniah may very well have been the editorial hand who arranged the oracles for posterity.

The Day of the Lord

Some scholars have noted that Zephaniah's personal relationship to the royal court inhibited him from making pronouncements against the royal administration. Whatever comforts and position his royal descent may have afforded him, he did not feel the need to be an advocate on behalf of the poor, a role most of the prophets took quite seriously. Nonetheless, Zephaniah wrote compellingly and with vigor about the judgment upon the sin he believed to be the cause of all of Judah's problems, lack of faith in God.

The imminence of doom is a strong theme in Zephaniah as he repeats warnings that "the day of the Lord is at hand." (1:7) "On that day" God will punish. (1:9) "On that day" cries will be heard from the Fish Gate and the Second Quarter. (1:10) "At that time" God will search out Jerusalem to find those whom God should punish. (1:12). "The great day of the Lord," which is near is "hastening fast" and sounds "bitter." (1:14) There is no mistake about it, "that day" is "a day of wrath" and will be filled with doom and gloom for God's people. (1:15, 16)

Others are Doomed

The prophet is not unmindful of the fact that Judah is no more guilty than the nations around her and those who have been her enemies. They, too, shall experience the judgment of God. In satirical fashion, Zephaniah calls his people to retreat in humility (2:1-3) as they also witness the judgment of God upon the nations. "The tenant of the house of Judah," (2:7) that handful of faithful who trust the covenant of God, will be the ones for whom God seeks vengeance on behalf of his people. (2:8)

Hope abounds as the prophet assures the people that the God who must speak judgment and visit wrath upon Judah and all people has not changed in character. God is perfectly willing to bring God's people home and gather them from their dispersions (3:20). God will renew them in love, (3:17) assist them in calling on the name of the Lord and in serving the Lord. (3:9) The whole matter of their rebellion is put behind in God's efforts on their behalf (3:11) and the removal of judgment. (3:15) All of this holds rich in promise to make the people of God renowned among the peoples of the earth when God restores their futures. (3:20)

A Paradigm

The Book of Zephaniah is a paradigm of the prophetic message and task. The prophet calls for repentance but warns the people of impending doom if they fail to change their ways. The prophet also feels compelled to speak judgment upon all nations who must be forced to acknowledge the kingship of God over all peoples. No matter how things work out, God will never renege on the promises God has made to Israel. They can always return in faith and God will make a new day for them. Thus there always will be a remnant who believe and to whom God can look that God might change the time from a day of wrath to a day of grace.

6. Nahum

THE PROPHET OF JUSTICE

We know nothing about the prophet Nahum, and we cannot even be certain about the town Elkosh, from which he came. (1:1) However, we do know that he came from Judah and that he prophesied sometime before the fall of Nineveh, the capital of Assyria, in 612 B.C. We can surmise that Nahum foretold the fall of the great city sometime near its destruction, so it is safe to suggest that he ministered in a time frame between 625-612 B.C.

The occasion for Nahum's "Oracle Concerning Nineveh" (1:1) was the dramatic decline in the influence of the city of Nineveh, the capital of Assyria. The city had been the center of Assyrian power for centuries. However, the death of Asshur-banipal, about 630 B.C., marked a turning point. Harrassed by enemies from the north and the south, the Assyrian power began to wane. Those who had been intimidated by Assyrian power could relax somewhat.

An Enthusiastic Reaction

The prophet Nahum reacted to the debilitating effect of the Assyrian domination with greater intensity than those who simply saw a change in the balance of political power. In a vision Nahum witnessed the imminent fall of the once proud city as the inevitable outcome of God's judgment upon a people who had plotted against the Lord. (1:9) Assyria was one more case history of a people who dared to be an adversary of God (1:2) only to have God make them "a gazingstock" (2:5, 6) before the nations of the earth.

37

No one could have celebrated the prospect of Nineveh's fall with greater enthusiasm. The fall of Nineveh would furnish the clinical proof that God "will make a full end of his adversaries and will pursue his enemies into darkness." (1:8) God had tolerated the evil of this people long enough. Their day in the sun was now over.

A Typical Case History

Nahum was convinced that God is a jealous God who was working out vengeance upon an adversary. (1:2) God's patience was not a flaw in God's behavior. God rather "is slow to anger and of great might, and the Lord will by no means clear the guilty." (1:3) However, in the future God will not have to bother with this enemy again, (1:9) because God will literally bury them. (1:14)

The prophet is so filled with indignation at the war crimes and oppression of Nineveh, the "bloody city all full of lies and booty" as well as plunder, that Nahum fails to issue a call to repentance on the part of his own people. The assumption is that Judah can learn from this piece of history. This was not an isolated instance of God's judgment upon a great city. God had used Assyria itself to destroy Thebes, the proud capital of Egypt. Was Nineveh any "better than Thebes" that she could escape this judgment? (3:8)

According to Plan

Nahum employed colorful, vigorous language to depict the fall of a ruthless people who defied the Lord of History. The first chapter of this book appears to have been an acrostic poem which would reflect the deep seated notion of the prophet that the judgment on the city of Nineveh was according to plan. In the destruction of the city God revealed God's determined plan to rid the earth of the enemies of God's people.

The theological import of Nahum's oracle against Nineveh rises no higher than the fundamental lesson that those nations which war against the Lord are doomed. They are passing references to the fact that the Lord is good to those who flee to him in the day of trouble (1:7) and that Judah can take heart, (1:15) "because God is restoring the majesty of Jacob." (2:2) After all, Judah had waited a long time for this day. Judah needed to be reminded of this truth that they were those who could still take refuge in him. (1:7)

7. Habakkuk

THE PROPHET OF FAITH

The prophet Habakkuk was one who raised serious questions about the violence to which God appeared to be indifferent. So distressed was the prophet that he entered into dialogue with God in which he complained about the way God was governing in the world. (1:2—2:5)

The violence Habakkuk had reference to is not identified. He does not specify the occasion. Habakkuk served in the seventh century B.C. He lived at a time when the moral corruption among his own people was very great. It was also a time when the super powers around his own nation posed imminent threats to his people. Habakkuk may have been railing against the disorders among his own people or complaining about the harrassments of the enemies of Judah. His complaints are so general as to make them applicable to all the violence.

Violence, according to the prophet, has its own rationale. (1:40) Violent people are absolutely mindless. (1:3) Violence appears to have no sensitivities and seems to be absolutely unreasonable. (1:7) They have taken matters into their own hands. They rely upon their own resources. They are confident that their best and most helpful resource is their own strength. They are determined to achieve their own goals, which they may not consider selfish at all, at their own costs. (1:11)

How Long?

Violence is the means of ruthless people who must have their own way. Violence can be the show of powerful people who want to prove the extent of their power. Meanwhile, the

41

people who believe in peace and goodwill among people have a great difficulty accepting the fact that violence can break out in so many places, last so long, hurt so many people, and appear to have its way so often. Those were exactly the sentiments of Habakkuk. As a man of God he tried to make some sense out of the message that God expected him to preach. If he was telling the people to get their own houses in order, the answer from the people may have been more violence. Or if he was trying to tell them that all would go right with them, the enemies may have been putting a hole in that drum.

Habakkuk felt all alone in his convictions. So he complains. How long is this situation supposed to continue without help from God? How long before God will save and rescue the situation? How long is he supposed to be witness to all of this trouble? All he sees is strife and contention.

Wait!

The prophet looks for an answer to his questions which he addressed to God. He takes his place on the watchtower where he apparently did receive some form of communications. Somehow God revealed himself in a word or vision to the prophet at this place. This time the prophet has determined that he will not leave the place until he has received a response to his complaints. He is not disappointed. A plain word does come from God. Habakkuk is to receive the message and share it by writing in large letters on some kind of billboard. The letters are to be large enough so that a runner who is passing by would be able to read it without stopping. Whoever is out jogging should be able to see it and make good sense out of it. (2:1-3)

The instruction about the message as to its time line is that it will come in due time. It may seem that the message is slow in arriving. It would appear that there is a delay to the message. It may feel as though it is never going to arrive. However, the message is more sure than anything else. It will come.

It is on the way. It is reliable. It will surely come. It will come in its own time. And when it does it will hasten to the end. There could hardly be any more assurance given than the word would definitely arrive in due time. At the same time God is conscious of the fact that this will also appear dreadfully slow to anyone who is waiting for a quick and hurried answer. It is the same word that one hears over and over again from the Hebrew prophets and psalmists, "Wait. Wait."

A Good Word

In the end, that is not how the prophet sees it. The message that Habakkuk receives from the Lord is one that he is willing to trust. If the prophet must wait, wait he will. He comes to the conclusion that there are two kinds of people in the world, those who are willing to take matters into their own hands. Those who take matters in their own hands are the ones who are causing the violence in the world. They are the disruptive ones. The bottom line is this, "Behold, he whose soul is not upright in him shall fail, but the righteous shall live by his faith." (2:4) When you shake it all down those who resort to the violence for whatever reason are going to fail if their hearts are not upright. If the causes of the violence do not serve the purposes of God, they are doomed.

On the other hand, "the righteous shall live by his faith." The one who is righteous is the one who is right with God. One is right with God because one trusts God. One trusts God, because God will do what has to be done. God does it in his own way and his own time. There is so little we know about God and how he does things that there is no way in which we can predict the hour, the day and the manner in which he will do his own thing. Yet we do know that God will do it. God will accomplish that which he pleases. It is knowing that which pleases us.

It's True

What the prophet says is true, because God showed how it all works out in the life of our Lord Jesus Christ. Our Lord himself was One who had to wait on the Lord. He had to wait on the Father. He endured the ridicule, the mockery, the hatred, the pain and the violence inflicted upon him by the world. The three hours that encompassed an eternity, he waited on the cross. In the Garden he had agonized for another eon of misery. Everything up to that moment had been testing and waiting time. At his baptism and at the transfiguration a word had come telling him to wait. But there was no word on the cross. Yet Jesus trusted, and God delivered him from the bitter pains of death.

Now we are also justified by our faith in the holy and living God who sent his own Son as our Savior. It is by faith in him that we can live and we shall not be disappointed. The Apostle Paul and Martin Luther were the ones who understood all the possibilities of what Habakkuk wrote. We say now that this trust is the cornerstone of our faith. And so it is. In the world of violence and death, we can be certain and sure that our God will make his word prevail, a word by which we can live, so while there is violence in the streets, we do not have to wonder what the world is coming to. We know. We know that our God will come. And we live by that faith, for it is right, and that is what makes us righteous.

8. Jeremiah

THE EMOTIONAL PROPHET

What we know as the Book of Jeremiah is really a collection of his sermons, poems, oracles and historical notes about him gathered by one or more of his admirers. The materials are not arranged chronologically or logically. They are pasted together as poorly as some family photo albums. Yet we know more about the life and person of this prophet than any other.

Jeremiah was born at the end of Manasseh's reign in Anathoth, a small village four miles northeast of Jerusalem on the edge of the wilderness. His father, Hilkiah, was the village priest. (1:1) Since he was from a priestly line, his ancestors had also been priests. Jeremiah was not yet twenty years old when God called him into his service as a prophet (726 B.C.). From the very beginning Jeremiah resisted that call and was most reluctant to enter upon the roll for which he felt himself inadequate and unprepared, not alone too youthful. (1:6, 7) Yet the call of God prevailed, and God brought Jeremiah into the role of prophet in spite of his protestations and resistance.

Jeremiah was the classic example of the prophet not being understood by his contemporaries. Some of his trials and persecutions were caused by members of his own family. Others were forced on him by other priests and prophets. (Chapter 28) Rulers and princes also fought against him. Nor was Jeremiah popular with the people. They also harassed him and made life so miserable for him he had to remain a celibate. (16:1-4) However, the greatest trial for Jeremiah was that he felt deeply the real miseries of his people and suffered greatly for their sake.

An Ex-Con

On occasion Jeremiah was imprisoned for his preaching. Jeremiah had been preaching to the people that God would visit judgment upon them and deliver them into the hands of the Babylonian Empire. Because of this bold preaching, Pashhur, a priest of the temple who served as chief officer of the temple, had Jeremiah thrown into prison. (20:1, 2) Jeremiah was undaunted by such action against him. To him it was another sign that the people would be visited with terror from every side. In fact Jeremiah told Pashhur that his name should be "Terror on Every Side." (2:3)

No legal action or punitive move against Jeremiah was going to prevent God's punishment for Jerusalem. All the cities and towns would be brought to final and complete destruction and even the temple would be in ashes. There was no way in which Jeremiah could be made to say what the people and his colleagues wanted to hear him say. He had to deliver to them what it was that God had revealed clearly. That, of course, is the base for the prophetic office. The prophet cannot deliver simply what is popular with the people, what is attractive to the people. The prophet cannot utter only that which draws a crowd or pleases the masses. Jeremiah was very clear on that point, and he was thoroughly consistent in remaining faithful to what God had asked him to deliver to the people. He could not bend or alter the Word from God to evoke from the people the kind of reaction that would make him a successful prophet. Faithful to that, however, he did react bitterly to God Himself. (Chapter 12)

The Problem with God

Jeremiah's struggle was not with the officers of the government, nor with the church, nor with the people. He felt the ongoing struggle with God. "O Lord, thou hast deceived me, and I was deceived; thou art stronger than I and thou hast prevailed." (20:7) The language suggests the frustrations of a deceived lover. Like a woman who has been deceived by a lover, the prophet complains to God that he has taken advantage of the prophet. God has simply satisfied his own purpose with the prophet and used him for his own will. The prophet can only mutter again and again that he had struggled against God for this whole business, and wanted no part of this doing, but he was too weak for God. God had overpowered him and won. But what was there in it for the prophet? What was the reward for being faithful to God's love? He had permitted himself to be used by God to speak the word, but no one would hear this word. He expected some good to come of what he was doing for God, but results were absolutely zero. He had believed that God was able to accomplish something through the word, but at the moment he could see nothing. (15:15-19) He believed that God's Word would not return void, but for now he had come up empty-handed.

Jeremiah did not mind being a part of God's delivery system. He did not mind being the mouthpiece for God. He did not mind being God's errand boy. However, now that he had been all that, it turned out that he served time in the stocks. But worse than that now he was the whipping boy for the whole population. "I have become a laughingstock all the day; everyone mocks me." (20:7) The prophet is a joke. No one wants to take him seriously at all. Yet they will not leave it go at that. They take the occasion and the opportunity to poke fun at him. The Word of God provokes that kind of response from those who do not want to believe it. People are so apathetic that they do not even want to hear it. However, the greater trouble comes from those who are close to the Word, who have heard expounded what the implications of the Word are, but do not want to accept them. They can never let it go at that. They feel compelled to react in some way that makes the prophet illegal, places him outside the religious community or simply mocks him. That Jeremiah was regarded as a joke undoubtedly had many twists to it. Some may have said that he had a demon, or that he was out of his mind, or that he simply was not with it. Jokes are made out of things that bother people most. Jeremiah could find no consolation in that. He just knew that the people had made him the laughing stock, but for him it was no laughing matter.

One Thing To Do

Jeremiah was not looking for sympathy. His sympathy was with God. In spite of all that happened to him, Jeremiah could not hold in the Word of God. He knew what kind of price he had to pay. His friends, relatives and superiors will accuse him again of being a spy from Babylon. They will say he is on the other side. (16:5-15) They will look for times when they can trip him up. They will watch for his fall. They will use any excuse they can to shut him up or to bring him to trial again. But in the face of all that, the prophet knows that he must get out this Word which burns like a fire in his bones. What a dilemma to be in! Already despised and a joke in the community, he knows that he will be worse off after he delivers the Word that is itching to get out. Jeremiah knows there is no other way. He must speak out the Word and let the results be what God permits or wants them to be. The prophetic role is seen for what it must be. It has only one prerogative. Be faithful to God.

Yet Jeremiah always finds comfort in God. Jeremiah knew that as sure as he had the Word from God, he was right, the people were wrong, other priests were wrong, other prophets were wrong, the king was wrong. Other people who handled the Word of God were wrong. Other people who prayed were wrong. But he knew that he would be vindicated. It would not be in his lifetime. But from here to eternity people would remember the Babylonian captivity that Jeremiah the prophet predicted. It will be to the eternal discredit of the people, and the name of Jeremiah would abide through eternity. (17:5-18)

Jeremiah had begun his ministry during the reign of Josiah, the king of Judah. Josiah was killed in the battle of Meggido by Pharaoh Necho and his Egyptian army in 609 B.C. Josiah,

48

who had instituted good temple reform, was succeeded by his son Jehoiakim, whom Necho made a puppet king. Jehoiakim was a cruel, sensuous and ineffectual king. During his reign, when the royal court was filled with intrigue and corruption, the people languished for the lack of good guidance.

The Temple Sermon

Sometime early in this period, Jeremiah went to the temple and preached a famous "Temple Sermon" (Chapters 7 and 26) in which he denounced the sins of his day, called for repentance and foretold the doom of his people if they did not repent. He made it clear that there would be no hiding behind the comfortable traditions and institutions of the temple as a protection from the doom that awaited them. Jeremiah left no holds barred. He refused to hold back anything from his people. He refused to offer any kind of false comfort or consolation for them in the face of this impending doom. He told the people that God would destroy the temple in the same way that Shiloh had been destroyed in the Northern Kingdom. Jeremiah had no difficulty saying this to the people, because the evidence was already in. The people had made no effort to reform their ways, and the enemies were already poised for action and growing in their power. The result was obvious. It was as plain as $2 + 2 = 4$.

Specifically Jeremiah said that, because there was no evidence of repentance, God was raising up Babylon to be God's servant to punish Judah. God was raising up a heathen nation that worshipped false gods to punish the people who believed that they were godly. Not only that, but Jeremiah saw that if there was to be no repentance the people should simply surrender to the hands of the enemy rather than to invite complete destruction. On top of that, when Jeremiah said that the people could not hide behind the presence of the temple, that was the same as saying they could not rely on the presence of God. The temple in Jerusalem was the shrine of Jahweh. The temple guaranteed the presence of God. To say the temple would be destroyed was the same as saying God would desert Judah.

Jeremiah drew a large audience. However, the audience was hostile and angry. The priests and the prophets warned Jeremiah that he would die, because he had dared to prophesy in God's name that the temple would be destroyed and the city annihilated. (26:7) Then someone informed the attendants at the royal court, and they came racing from the statehouse to seize him and bring him to trial for what they regarded as high treason. (26:10)

The final outcome of this scene was that Jeremiah had just enough friends in the court that his life was spared for the moment. Some of those who held court positions and enough of the people spoke on his behalf, so that no action was taken against him at that time. Some of the elders rose to Jeremiah's defense by pointing out that other great prophets had been spared when they had brought unwelcome words from the Lord. (26:16-19)

However, Jeremiah did not enjoy peace for long. His detractors continued to make life miserable for him. Some of the people who were his accusers were priests and prophets. Jeremiah scolded them and asked, "How can you say, 'We are wise and the Word of the Lord is with us?' But behold the false pen of the scribes has made it into a lie." (8:8) He also thundered, "Do not trust in these deceptive words: 'This is the temple of the Lord, the temple of the Lord, the temple of the Lord.' " (7:4) Anyone can throw around the Word of God for one's own purposes. However, one could know that the word which is preached, written, or is taught is not a lie when the bottom line of that word is a call for faith in a God who is willing to save and redeem his people purely by his grace and love. These people were trying to save themselves by their treaties, their intrigues, and by their own devices. That is why Jeremiah said they could not do it. Better they surrender. (Chapter 27) They should return to the God who had fashioned them like a potter who fashions his vessels. (18:5-12) They should trust this God who was willing to make a new covenant with them in the same way that he had made a covenant with their fathers. (31:31-35)

True To the End

Jeremiah never relinquished his position. At the very first confrontation he made clear his position. He announced that it was the Lord who had sent him to deliver the message he had. He called them to repentance so that God could withhold the threatened punishment. If they refused, he argued, they could do with Jeremiah whatever they wished. However, if they put him to death, they would have added to their guilt and brought innocent blood upon the city. Jeremiah won that round as far as his own safety was concerned. However, the situation did not improve and Jeremiah had to go down in Hebrew history as the "Weeping Prophet," because of the many tears he had to shed for the city that refused to repent. What happened in the life of Jeremiah in the end, we are not sure.

When Babylonia did come to take over the city, Jeremiah urged the people to stay and suffer what they might at the hands of their enemies, rather than go down to Egypt. Jeremiah believed the exile was necessary to bring Judah to repentance. The leaders were enraged at him and carried him off to Egypt. (Chapters 42-44) He had suffered much at their hands in imprisonment. Now he suffered greater indignities. What his life was like in Egypt we are not sure. Tradition has it that he was stoned to death in Egypt. There is no final word on that, but that may have been his fate. His entire ministry had been marked by strange behavior, because the people had so clearly rejected him and made him something of a social outcast. Because he was so regarded, Jeremiah himself resorted to bizarre and parabolic behavior to illustrate that while he was rejected by them, it was God who would ultimately reject them because of their unbelief. He used a waist cloth to make the point, (Chapter 13) made the potter an illustration, (Chapters 18 and 19) used baskets of figs and a vial of wine as paradigms of what was happening. However, he also purchased a field as an assurance that God would restore his people. (Chapter 32)

Jeremiah wept, prayed and suffered for Judah. He was prophet, mediator and vicarious sufferer for his people. He confessed to his pain and openly wept and mourned for Jerusalem. (Chapters 14 and 15) Later another prophet was to come to Jerusalem and weep for her in the person of the Lord Jesus Christ. He, too, would suffer and die for her, and in so doing fulfill the new covenant prophesied by Jeremiah. (31:31-35)

9. Ezekiel

THE VISIONARY

Ezekiel was born to the priestly family of Buzi living in Jerusalem. (1:3) He was a boy when Jeremiah was a prophet preaching to the people preceding the fall of Jerusalem to the Babylonians. That must have been difficult for a lad to hear. The children of Jerusalem must have been impressed as their parents discussed the preaching of this prophet Jeremiah, who called the people to repentance and predicted the fall of Jerusalem. The parents resisted the word of the prophet and thought of him as one in sympathy with the enemy. The children may have been terrified at the prospect of losing to an enemy. That must have been especially true for the young Ezekiel, who was identified with a family that found its livelihood woven into the life of the temple worship in the holy city.

As a pious lad, which Ezekiel evidently was, he must have been especially sensitive to any judgment that had to be made against the people whom he knew to be the chosen of God. From his writings it is apparent that Ezekiel was no heady intellectual. Rather he was that kind of person who felt keenly and reflected his emotional state. His writings are colorful and filled with pathos. They are the writings of one who has that kind of emotional radar that picks up the vibes of everyone and everything around.

The writings are problematic for interpretation, because they are cast in the language of the vision not too unlike the Book of Revelation. Such writings usually are best understood by people living in bondage, duress, or in concentration camps. For them the symbolic language is filled with hope and promise.

A D.P.

Ezekiel was one of those carried off into captivity in the first wave of people deported to Babylon before the final destruction of Jerusalem (597 B.C.). He must have greeted the call to be a prophet with distressed feelings in that time of great personal turbulence. If Ezekiel had been depressed by what he saw, heard and experienced as a lad, he was shocked by the manner in which the call from God (1:1—3:15) came to him in an esoteric vision of heavenly angels and a wheel. The call presented no happy prospect for him. He heard the voice speak to him, "Son of man, I send you to the people of Israel, to a nation of rebels, who have rebelled against me."

The complaint was that this generation and those previous had rebelled against God. (2:3) They continued to be obstinate and imprudent. The prospects for any changes are slim. The call was stated in such a way the assumption was that the people are not likely to hear. No reason was stated for a quick change of heart. No encouragement was offered that the people will be warmed by what the prophet has to say. There was no promise of any kind of success. In fact, the opposite was predicted. Even if the prophet sits among briars and thorns and upon the scorpions of the people, he is not to be afraid of their words. The prophet was told that he can expect abuse from the people. He could expect that the people would behave as an enemy. The people whom he was sent to save were the people who would be out to destroy him. This was not the cruel, hard world out there who do not believe in God. The description was of people who are supposedly the people of God.

No Snow Job

It is significant that all this was spelled out so clearly for the prophet in his call. The prophet did not receive a snow job. There were no incentives held out to him. He was not told how much cooperation there would be on the parts of committees and officers in the congregation. He was not encouraged by promises of all that the people will do for him. He was told only that the Word which he will deliver to the people will be true in spite of how tough the people make it for him. He is told that no matter how mean the people will look to him the Word which he delivers from God will be the Word of God. The Word of God does not depend upon the acceptance of people. That Word is real, honest and trustworthy whether the people hear or refuse to hear it. In the parlance of the prophet that means whether they believe and obey it, or whether they do not. The trustworthiness of the Word of God does not depend upon success. The proof for the Word of God being among people is not whether the prophet can draw an audience or not. God's Word stands fast among peoples who refuse to listen, to be diligent about it or not.

In spite of the mean prospects for him in this calling, Ezekiel served as the prophet of God for the people of Israel. He came to understand that his calling was to faithfulness and not to success. Before the final fall of Jerusalem he reflected a high sense of doom for his people. They were as useless as the wood of the grapevine that the carpenter must discard in the fire. (Chapter 15) For six years his preaching was filled with warning, correction and foreboding. (Chapters 1-24) But just as certainly as he remained faithful to God's Word, the people were as unrepentant as God had predicted and invited their own disaster. They were like an unfaithful wife. (Chapters 16 and 23)

The Highs and the Lows

Over and over again Ezekiel laments the fact that the people fail to recognize that it is God who regulates the world powers. When mighty Babylon showed its strength and made a pact with Israel, the covenant put Israel in the position of a servile state. At the same time the covenant granted Israel protection. Israel broke the covenant by trying to make a treaty with Egypt as a defense. The prophet reasons that this was a serious error. To break a covenant with Babylon was to invite disaster. Babylon was the stronger of the nations, and Israel had betrayed its own weakness by relying upon the strength of another power that was too weak to be of help. However, the prophet's main argument is that as certainly as Israel had broken the covenant with Babylon, it had committed the greater sin of breaking covenant with God. That was Israel's mistake. God would therefore now take this nation into captivity in Babylon where they could reflect upon their trespasses. In the process many would fall and those that remained would be scattered to the winds, and all would know that it was at the hand of God that all had taken place.

In a prophetic oracle the prophet pictures a tender twig of a high cedar planted on a mountain top to create a high cedar once more. (17:22-24) Then, "All the trees of the field shall know that I the Lord bring low the high tree, and make high the low tree, dry up the green tree, and make the dry tree flourish. I the Lord have spoken, and I will do it." (17:24) What the oracle speaks of is God's kingly rule. This is how God establishes his kingdom among people. He is speaking here of how he regulates the highs and lows of his people. This is what God did with Israel. The oracle clearly suggests that eleven other "trees of the field" that is, all governments, shall recognize the hand of God in what he is doing for his people. The general theme of the prophet is that God regulates the high and the low in all the nations. In Chapters 25-32 the prophet speaks oracles against seven nations.

Who Could Believe?

It was difficult for Israel to accept his prophetic message. No one wanted to believe that God was raising this super power Babylon against his chosen Israel. If Israel were God's people, it made more sense to believe that God was on their side to protect and defend against all mortal enemies. The notion that a nation like Babylon that did not worship the true God Jahweh could be the servant of Jahweh did not make sense. The prophet did not simply predict that nation would rise against nation, but that God would raise nation against nation. God raises the high and the mighty. God does not simply permit evil to happen and then picks up the pieces. The prophetic word is that God raises up the high and mighty Babylon to be God's servant against the people of Israel. God is not simply a spectator to history but is actively engaged in what goes on in the world of highs and lows.

Israel also had a difficult time managing the notion that God should bring his own people low. Israel was not totally unaware that they were sinners. They had not stopped worshiping. They had not sinned much more than other nations. Israel still had the temple, still had priests, still made sacrifices, still had prophets. It was inconceivable that Israel should be brought low and others exalted when the sins of others were so much more obvious.

A Great Hope

The thrust of the prophet's message, however, was one of great hope. God still did what the prophetic oracle promised. God created the highs and the lows. He brought life out of death. God established the kingdom of grace in the midst of earthly kingdoms and powers. History itself demonstrates the incapability of people to learn from previous generations. Yet it is for the people of God to discern in history what God is doing. They do so not by reason, but by faith.

The manner in which God deals with all the nations is the assurance that God would preserve Israel. God would in time destroy the others, and no longer would these nations hurt Israel, (28:24) and God had delivered their fathers out of Egypt. (29:32-44) In spite of the fact that the rulers to whom God had entrusted the people failed in their roles as shepherds, God would serve as Shepherd to the people to seek the lost, bring back the strayed, heal them, and strengthen them. (Chapter 34) In the dramatic vision of the valley of the dry bones (37:1-14) the prophet sees that all hope rests in God alone who is able to breathe life back into these people who had been dead.

God's renewal of the covenant with Israel would be forever, David would be King, and they should dwell in the land forever in the presence of God. (37:24-28) On the twenty-fifth anniversary of his exile Ezekiel is transported in a vision to a high mountain in Israel from which he has a vision of the new temple. (Chapters 40-42) Israel could anticipate that the new temple would be the place where God would dwell. This would be "the most holy place," (41:7) the shrine from which God would direct the lives of Israel. "The glory of the Lord entered the temple by the gate facing east." (43:4) Once more the ordinances in God's house would signal that all things are restored for God's people (Chapters 44-46) and the presence of God and divine blessings are guaranteed by the river flowing from the temple, God's throne. (47:1-12) Ezekiel shared these great hopes with the exiles as they languished in Babylon. They could be confident that God would destroy the enemy Gog of Magog, and gain the final victory. (Chapters 38, 39) In that day God's greatness and holiness would be recognized by many nations and they would know God is Lord (38:23) and when Jerusalem and the new temple are rebuilt after Israel's penitential exile, then the people shall know the name of the city as "The Lord is there." (48:35)

10. Isaiah

THE POET(S) OF HOPE

Hope for the exiles in Babylon was offered in the poetry and hymnody of chapters 40-66 of Isaiah. The anonymous author of chapters 40-55 is commonly called Second Isaiah.

Second Isaiah ministering about 550-540 B.C. broke through the gloom of the exile to announce the restoration of God's people when God sends Cyrus to engineer the fall of Babylon. (44:28) The call comes to Second Isaiah that he is to announce that Israel's "iniquity is pardoned" (40:2) and that she should be comforted with the good news which should prepare her for the new day of the Lord. (40:1-8)

Had God Forgotten?

The prophet had great sympathy for God's people who were still in exile. It was sad enough that they bore the onus of being a banished people. They had lost their status as a nation. Their capital city back home was in ruins. Their national shrine had been desolated. Some of their people still languished in poverty there. Whatever privileges they enjoyed in Babylon were diminished by the fact that they were ruled by an alien people. Over and over again they had to ask themselves if there was any way out of their present dilemma. Whatever they knew of their history was a monotonous account of ineptitude among the great powers of the world. Their fathers before them had been delivered from slavery in Egypt only to be humiliated by one foe after another. For two generations in exile they entertained few hopes of deliverance by some heroic figure who could come and deliver them. As the psalmist told it they wept by the rivers of Babylon for the ill fortunes that had overcome them. In this depressed condition how could they entertain the notion that the God of the Hebrews had any concern for them. If God had banished them to this foreign land had he not forsaken them forever?

Remember the God of Old

The prophet suggests that at such a moment the captives could think of the way in which God had dealt with his people before. God had found them in this predicament originally. When the Israelites had been in slavery in Egypt, God had intervened for them. Then the Lord made "a way in the sea, a path in the mighty waters." (43:16) God made a way of escape for his people when he led them through the Red Sea. God also brought down the armies of Pharaoh for his people. He quenched out that entire army of chariots, horses and warriors. He drowned them in the sea and they never rose from it. He did all of that as simply as snuffing out the wick of a candle. So if God did it once, could he not do it again for his people? That would be simple enough. He ought to be able to lead his people out of Babylon and deliver them safely into their homeland. Certainly the prophets had referred back to this great incident of God's providence and salvation for his people over and over again when their people had faced difficulty. The Exodus was the great sign of God's compassion and mercy for his people. It had been the word from the past that was also the word for whatever they had to face in their future. God was with them and would go with them again.

The memory of what God had done for his people was valuable and important. The rehearsal of that salvation history of God's people was an assurance of God's capability and his presence. It was all of that and much more. It was one of those mighty acts of God which insure his goodness and grace for his people. However, the prophet says that God does not want the people to rely upon the past alone. That was notable, to be sure. Yet people can get to the point that they believe God did his thing only in the past. They can come to the conclusion that God does not work that way anymore.

Such attitudes may have colored much of the conversation of the exiles while they were in Babylon. It was difficult for them to get some comfort out of the Exodus that had happened centuries before for the benefit of their ancestors, and at the same time trying to find some meaning in that event for themselves.

Watch What God Can Do

In response to that the prophet says God instructs, "Remember not the former things, nor consider the things of old. Behold, I am doing a new thing now and it springs forth, do you not perceive it?" (44:18, 19) This is God's way of saying to the people, "You think I did well in the past? You haven't seen anything yet!" It was also calling attention to the fact that God had not laid down his tools. God was not out of the contemporary picture. God was ready to do for these people as he had done for their forebears. In fact, he was doing it already. He was giving them a new deal.

The exiles could not see what was happening. The prophet was mindful of the fact that the power of Babylonia was beginning to wane. He saw Cyrus building the Assyrian Empire's strength. He knew the prudence of that ruler. He was sure he would be a servant of God who would deliver the exiles from their imprisonment. What was happening in history was under the control of the Almighty. And what God would affect would be radical changes for the sake of his people. If he opened a path in the Red Sea before, he would make rivers flow in the deserts now. All the stubborn wild beasts of the wilderness would also have to acknowledge his honor. God would feed his chosen people and give them occasion to declare his praise when he delivers them.

The prophet was right. At that very moment God was setting the stage for the deliverance of the exiles. Cyrus did expand his power, overtook Babylon, and permitted the exiles to return home under protection. It was one more mighty act of God performed for the benefit of his people so that they could discern in all that he did for them the pattern of their salvation.

Good as His Word

Second Isaiah is sent by that word of God which stands forever. (40:8) This is the same word by which God had called, shaped, ruled the people and the world (45:22, 23) and by which he would continue to shape the future and the special destiny of his people. (55:6-13)

God could be trusted again. (40:12-31) God ruled not only the affairs of the people of Israel through thick and thin, but all peoples could test and see how God rules the earth, for who else would know that God was the one to "stir up one from the north?" (Chapter 41) The same God who created the heavens and the earth, and rules in the earth over all things is the Redeemer God of Israel who remains unchallenged by all other gods in the earth. (Chapters 42-44)

God Incomparable

This sovereign, incomparable God who demonstrates the futility of other gods, elects Cyrus of Persia a king alien to God's people, to be the shepherd to lead Israel out of exile. (44:28) Cyrus is God's "anointed" one, God's savior to "subdue nations" for the sake of God's people, even when Cyrus knows not God or God's purpose. (45:1-17) Israel should awaken to the restoration God has prepared for her with the downfall of Babylon, (Chapter 46) which indicated that God was doing for the beloved what God had always done as the Redeemer of Israel. (Chapters 47-49) God had never been divorced from his beloved and the hand of God had not been shortened that God could not redeem. (Chapter 50) God would deliver the people speedily, and God's salvation would endure forever. (Chapter 51)

Interspersed in these chapters are dialogues God conducts with the nation Israel and other gods as well as the well-known Servant Songs which have received considerable comment. (42:1-4, 49:1-6, 50:4-9, 52:13—53:12) The servant is not identified in the poems, so some have concluded they are the autobiographical notes of Second Isaiah. Others see the Servant as Israel. Christians, by and large, have little difficulty seeing the Servant Songs as descriptions of all that Jesus of Nazareth accomplished for us by his passion, death and resurrection.

Second Isaiah closes his book of poetry on the positive note that the unfathomable gracious God whose ways are higher than ours would not permit the word of promise and hope to return void. (Chapter 55)

A New Day

Chapters 56-66 of Isaiah are of a different moment. The tone of these chapters is so different, some have attributed the material to a third Isaiah. The scene has changed. The exiles have returned under Cyrus, and now the people must be encouraged to return to the ways of the Lord. Justice must be restored and the house of God must be made a house of prayer for all peoples. (Chapter 56) All impediments and obstructions to true worship must be swept aside that the faithful may perform unselfish service to the needy and afflicted. (Chapters 57 and 58) Repentance is called for (Chapter 59) that God might vindicate the people. (Chapter 62) Chapter 64 is a prayer that God would give a revelation as in former days, and in the subsequent chapter (65) God answers that God had been willing, but the people had been silent.

Chapters 60, 61 and 63 are beautiful poems insuring the people that God has ushered in a new day of grace and providence for them. The poems are psalmodies celebrating the goodness of God which Christian believers see as fulfilled in the mission, ministry, suffering, crucifixion and going to the Father of Jesus. Concluding oracles (Chapter 66) end on the note that all flesh shall eventually come to worship before the Lord.

11. Obadiah

THE CLONE OF JEREMIAH

The name of the Prophet Obadiah means "Servant of Jahweh" or "Worshiper of Jahweh." The name is a common one among the Hebrew Scriptures. The pious governor in Ahab's house (1 Kings 18) was Obadiah, as were a prince at the time of Jehoshaphat (2 Chronicles 17:7) and a Levite who helped with the repairs to the temple under Josiah. (2 Chronicles 34:12) However, there is no way one can identify the Prophet Obadiah with any of these persons or any of the other nine characters who owned the same name which dubbed them as special servants of Jahweh.

A Familiar Message

It is clear that Obadiah served in Judah, but there is no way to establish with certainty when he prophesied. Rough estimates of the timing have placed the prophet in both pre-exilic and post-exilic periods. However, some clues within the text of Obadiah would strongly suggest that the material comes either from the late sixth or early to mid fifth century. Verses one to nine are close parallels to a piece in Jeremiah, (49:1-2) which would indicate that both may have employed a common source which was pre-exilic. Jeremiah uses the oracle as a prediction, whereas Obadiah makes the oracle an introduction for explaining why the destruction of Edom has taken place. Also the Prophet Joel has a number of phrases in chapter three that are common to Obadiah, and Joel 2:32 quotes Obadiah 17, suggesting that Obadiah precedes Joel. The evidence would place Obadiah sometime after the destruction of Jerusalem (587 B.C.) and before Joel who prophesied about 400 B.C.

The message of Obadiah is similar to the classical style of the prophets. The prophet examines the judgment which had befallen Edom as typical of the judgment which God will visit upon all the nations of the earth in the Day of the Lord. While all peoples must face the consuming judgment of this final reckoning, victory is promised to God's people, who have also been justly punished for their sins.

Restoration Will Come

The prophet makes special note of the fact that God employed the former allies of Edom (v. 7) to rout the Edomites (v. 1) and to completely pillage and plunder them. (vv. 5, 6) More judgment was yet to come (vv. 8-10), because the Edomite had been driven into southern Judea and had yet to be displaced from this territory as a judgment and revenge for their part in the destruction of Jerusalem. (vv. 10-16) Of course, the prophet is not so driven by his concern for the vengeance that God would visit upon Edom that he does not see this as a part of the larger judgment that will come "upon all nations." (v. 15) Like Edom all of them "shall be as though they had not been." (v. 16)

The people of God, however, can be certain "that in Mount Zion there shall be those who escape." (v. 17) The exiles shall be returned. The kingdom will be restored and the boundaries expanded. Once more the special people of God will be witness to the world that God rules over all peoples when this restoration will be complete. Then the "kingdom shall be the Lord's." (v. 21)

12. Haggai

THE RECONSTRUCTION PROPHET

The name of the Prophet Haggai means "Festal," which suggests that he was born on some Hebrew Festival. His parents undoubtedly accepted the celebrated birth as a sign that Haggai was destined for a special calling from God in service to God's people. If the Book of Haggai is the sum of the prophet's activity, we must assume that his career was a brief one that covered a period of a few months of 520 B.C., the second year of the rule of the Persian king Darius, who ruled 522-486 B.C. The timing of the utterances are precisely documented in the book. (1:1, 1:15, 2:1, 2:10 and 2:14) Since this prophetic ministry is so brief, we gain the impression that Haggai is an old man who has the memory of the house of God "in its former glory" (2:3) from pre-exilic days. With the confidence that God will once again bless the people with the divine presence if they rebuild the shrine for God, he gives encouragement for undertaking the task.

For the Right Time

The stimulation which Haggai offered for the rebuilding of the temple was desperately needed. Cyrus, the King of Persia, had conquered the Babylonian Empire in 539 B.C. As was his custom to accommodate the peoples he had conquered by granting them their religious freedom, Cyrus issued a decree that allowed the Hebrew exiles to return home. (Ezra 1:2-4) According to Ezra, (2:1, 2) some did return under this decree. However, for almost twenty years nothing was done to rebuild the temple. Apparently those who had not been in captivity continued to worship in the outdoors at the ruins of the temple. The returned exiles may have found that convenient also. Haggai noted that the people had felt that the time had "not yet come to rebuild the house of the Lord" (1:2) but the people had found time for building or reconstructing their homes. However, he also observed that prosperity had not yet come to Jerusalem, because God could not and would not bless them until they restored the shrine where God could once more dwell in glory. (1:7-11)

The encouragement that better times were in the offing when the people would sacrifice for the building of the temple was well received. Zerubbabel, a Babylonian Jew of the royal house of David and appointed Governor of Judah by Darius, the Persian King, and Joshua, the High Priest, collaborated to lead the people in the rebuilding of the temple. (2:14, 15) The initiation of the reconstruction of the house of God marked also the restoration of God's will toward the people. Not only would God once more bless them, "but the latter splendor of this house shall be greater than the former." God would give them prosperity, and the nations of the earth would be shaken and their treasures would come into the temple. (2:6-9)

Getting Priorities Straight

However, the prophet reminds the people that they are to take their places before God as a sanctified people. They could be and had been as defiled and unclean as those nations who knew not God. (2:10-14) Before the work of the rebuilding of the temple had begun, the people did not experience blessing upon their agricultural activity. Now that the temple foundation had been laid they could rely on God, who said, "From this day on I will bless you." (2:15-19) The prophet was not suggesting some low formula by which the temple was a shrine comparable to the fertility gods of the idolatrous nations around them. The rebuilding of the temple had been symbolic of a repentant attitude and a commitment to the God of Promise.

68

The future hope of Judah was in God's hands, and Haggai appeared to entertain the notion that God would use Zerubbabel as a servant to effect great changes. (2:20-23) Haggai may have envisioned Zerubbabel to be the Messianic King. "I will take you, O Zerubbabel, my servant, the son of Shealtiel, says the Lord, and make you like a signet ring; for I have chosen you." (2:23) The fate of Zerubbabel is unknown. He fades from the picture. He was never appointed king, but he and Joshua did get the temple built. In 1516 B.C., four years after Haggai made his first appeal, the temple was completed.

13. Zechariah

THE CHEERLEADER

The moment in which the prophet Zechariah served was not a happy one. These were post-Babylonian days. Exiles had returned to Babylon (537 B.C.) when Cyrus became king of Persia. The word of the prophets who had ministered in the days of the exile had come true. God had delivered and saved His people once more. However, the promised glorious days in Jerusalem did not return. The city was not rebuilt. The temple was still in ruins. There was no prosperity in the land. The people were not only poor and destitute economically, but they were now poor in spirit. There was no sign that the former glory would return to Jerusalem. There was no hope for the kingdom to be reestablished. What king would come on this scene of ruins and dashed hopes? There simply was no verve left, no spirit, no desire to rebuild. Unto this dreary scene comes the prophet Zechariah to challenge and encourage his people to take heart and to build. (520 B.C.) The prophet did his best to arouse the people and to spur them on to restore the city of God. The prophet had high hopes for these people, because they are God's chosen ones. God would give them the vigor and the energy to make Jerusalem His dwelling place once more.

Confidence

The prophet Zechariah was confident in the face of such hopeless conditions. The sign for him that things would change was God's track record. God had not forgotten his people, and God would not ignore his people now. In addition, Zechariah was sensitive to international events. There were

71

changes in the Persian Empire and rumblings on the international scene that gave promise that things would turn around under Darius, the new king in Persia. Furthermore, there was a figure who strode on the scene who gave some inkling that Israel might experience the restoration of the Davidic throne. That figure was Zerubbabel, a Babylonian Jew who returned to Jerusalem to rule as governor under Darius. (Chapter 4) Zerubbabel was a descendant of David and he enjoyed great prestige with Darius. There is a legend about him in the apocrypha book *I Esdras*. How much of that story is true is hard to decipher. Yet its prominence suggests to us how heroic a figure Zerubbabel was. The legend has it that three bodyguards of Darius created a contest among themselves to determine what is the strongest. The first said that wine was, and he gave the rationale for that opinion. The second argued how he believed that the king was strongest. The third, who was Zerubbabel, convincingly argued that women were stronger than either the wine or the king, but that the strongest of all was truth. Darius and his court approved unanimously of Zerubbabel's answer. In payment Darius rewarded Zerubbabel by granting his request to help the exiles in their return to rebuild Jerusalem.

A Second David

Zechariah was certain that it was this Zerubbabel who would come to restore the fortunes of Jerusalem, to restore the Davidic kingdom and throne, to usher in an era of peace, and to establish the rule that would truly be messianic. Unfortunately, Zerubbabel never rose to a position higher than that of governor. The Davidic throne was not reestablished. There is no evidence that the Persian rulers ever again appointed a governor from the house of David. Furthermore, Zerubbabel may have been removed from office and martyred, because of his refusal to cooperate completely with Persia. That suspicion is based on the fact that at the rededication of the temple Zerubbabel's name is missing. That is a glaring omission since he was so prominent and instrumental in the rebuilding of the temple. He had a tremendous impact on early post-Babylonian days, and he looms so large in Hebrew tradition and legend.

Zechariah never doubted that the people could regain the favor their ancestors had lost. The people could return to God in repentance, (1:3-6) because God had promised to cause prosperity to flow, to comfort Zion and again choose Jerusalem. (1:17) Over and over again he promises the presence of God who returns to Zion (8:3) and brings the people from east and west and renews the covenant with them. (8:7, 8) The proof will be when people from other nations grab hold of the robe of a Jew and say, "Let us go with you, for we have heard that God is with you." (8:23)

Another Voice

Chapters 9-14 of Zechariah were not from his hand. Some of the materials in those chapters are difficult to interpret. Some may have been pre-exilic and most of the material is difficult to date though they do reflect the restless character of the people in the centuries before Christ who envision a day of vengeance for the enemy and vindication for God's people. (Chapters 12-14) These materials were well known in the early Christian community and New Testament writers frequently quoted from these chapters to demonstrate their fulfillment in the person of Christ. The evangelists refer to the coming of the triumphant King (9:9) in Matthew 21:5 and John 12:15. The thirty shekels of silver (11:12-14) appear in Matthew 26:15, 27:9 and John 19;37. The pierced side (12:10) appears in Revelations 1:7, Matthew 26:31 and Mark 14:27. Once again the Christian community had no trouble in discovering how the prophetic word was fulfilled in Christ.

14. Ezra-Nehemiah

THE BUILDING PROPHETS

Ezra and Nehemiah, which appear to be the product of one author, may have been known originally as Ezra and later as 1 and 2 Ezra. In addition there are other materials known as 3 and 4 Ezra, which are not a part of the canon.

One Message

The books Ezra and Nehemiah are accounts of the return of Jewish exiles to Jerusalem from Babylonia. Ezra is pictured as the forceful scribe who inspired the spiritual reformation necessary for the rebuilding of the holy city, but more importantly, the restructuring of the remnant as the people of God. Nehemiah is the efficient and faithful personality who achieved administrative successes for completing the job of reordering Jerusalem. For both, the rebuilding of Jerusalem was for the purpose of reinstituting the temple and the cultic practices associated with the holy shrine as the center and heart of Jewish life.

Though the two books are named for Ezra and Nehemiah, they are not the authors. The author may have been the anonymous Chronicler, who also gave us 1 and 2 Chronicles. The argument has been advanced that the chronicler may have been Ezra himself. The author cites sources which include the memoirs of Nehemiah (Nehemiah 1:1) and the memoirs of Ezra (8:1-36), which appears to be the more compatible with the style and theology of the Chronicles. However, the Ezride authorship is not conclusive, because the entire work has all the earmarks of being edited sometime in the era 350-250 B.C., considerably later than the fifth century when Ezra and Nehemiah would have been active.

Faith is Required

The confused chronological arrangement in the two books has been explained by some as the editor's lack of information. Others attribute the bad mix in the materials to confusion in the transmission of the texts. What is significant is that a serious study of the texts calls into question any relationship between Ezra and Nehemiah. There is no indication of any awareness of mutual recognition of the two, and it is unlikely that the two came to Jerusalem at the same time. Nehemiah probably would have come first if he came to a desolate city, (Nehemiah 7:4) and Ezra would have come later if he worked in a busy and well populated city. (Ezra 10:1)

Ezra cannot be ranked among the great prophets. However, his reputed learning coupled with his intense piety reclaimed the prophetic message. He is credited with marshalling the resources of the exiles who came with him from Babylonia to Jerusalem. (Ezra 8:15-36) What is more noteworthy in Ezra was the reaction to what had brought the Hebrew people into exile in the first place. Ezra blushed with shame for the continuing flirtation of his people with other peoples in the land who were guilty with their "pollutions," "abominations," and "uncleanness." (Ezra 9:1-11) The remedy Ezra suggested has been judged as harsh and legalistic. Ezra contended that the only insurance the remnant had that they could once again claim the land was to make intermarriage with the people who "practice these abominations" taboo. (Ezra 9:12-15) God had intended the land for their eternal inheritance. The message was plain. The people could respond in obedience and faith. "Our God has not forsaken us in our bondage, but has extended to us his steadfast love before the kings of Persia, to grant us some reviving to set up the house of our God, to repair its ruins, and to give us protection in Judea and Jerusalem." (Ezra 9:9)

Building Community

Nehemiah is a layman and an eunuch, who is a cupbearer in the court of the Persian King Artaxerxes at Susa. He is not only granted leave to go to Jerusalem to organize the rebuilding of the city but he is eventually appointed governor in the land of Judah. He was successful in overcoming the opposition to the rebuilding of the walls, (4:1-23) effecting internal economies and reforms, (5:1-19) and reinstating the covenant with the people. (10:28-39) The record of memoirs of Nehemiah are generally regarded as accurate in chronology and substance.

Criticism of Ezra-Nehemiah is that the books are the source of a new nationalism, provincialism, and legalism that set the stage for creating the narrowness and bigotry that were characteristic of Judaism when our Lord came upon the scene. The criticism is hardly fair. The truth is that Ezra-Nehemiah is a record of how the people of Jerusalem were able to build community under adverse conditions in contrast to the poor record of their fathers under the kings. Ezra-Nehemiah was the work of the Chronicler, who took seriously the fact that the people of God would worship the God who alone could grant them peace and prosperity by grace. God had made that abundantly clear through prophets and the record of how God's people were when they listened or did not listen to the prophets. The Chronicler's theology was no different from the prophetic message that announced over and over again that when the people trust and obey the Word of God, they would be blessed, and if not, they would suffer. Perversions and distortions of these theological insights occur when people work them in reverse. When people believe that God must bless them, because they have worshiped or obeyed, they deny the very nature of God, who acts by divine initiative, who is "ready to forgive, gracious and merciful, slow to anger and abounding in steadfast love." (Nehemiah 9:17)

15. Joel

THE TEMPLE PROPHET

Almost nothing is known about the prophet Joel, whose name means "Jahweh is God," a name not uncommon in the Hebrew community. The prophet may have written sometime around the turn of the fifth century B.C., after the temple had been rebuilt in post-exilic times in the Persian period (539-331 B.C.). The occasion for the oracles collected in this book appears to be a horrendous plague of locusts. (Chapter 1) Joel sees in the devastation wrought by the locusts a judgment of God and a sign of future judgment. The plague is a warning that a darker day, "the day of the Lord," could befall them. (2:1, 2)

The Day of the Lord

Earlier commentators suggested that the plague of locusts was a description of the possible invasion of enemy armies. Naturalists, however, conclude that this is an accurate portrayal of the havoc caused by locusts. Students of literature are also ecstatic about the sheer poetry of the book and the vividness with which it pictures the phenomenon of the locusts. Joel was caught up in profound sympathy for the people who suffered much and had been so impoverished that some of them sold their children into slavery. (3:3) He felt badly for the wholesale destruction the people had experienced, but knew God could restore the losses. What chilled him, however, was that the catastrophe he witnessed was but a signal of how thorough and how complete the judgment of God could be. "The day of the Lord is great and very terrible; who can endure it?" (2:11)

The prophet believed that the dreadful circumstances in which the people found themselves could be changed radically if the proper relationship were established between God and the people. The people would have to return to the Lord. To return to the Lord was to repent. But what did these people have to repent of? These were the people who huddled around the temple to commiserate with one another and to look for comfort. They had not been irreligious and indifferent to worship. The religious establishment had not been shut down. However, the prophet calls their religiousity and their piety into question. In a stirring plea that has been a classic pericope for Ash Wednesday, (2:12-19) the prophet calls for a spiritual fast, "Yet even now," says the Lord, "return to me with all your heart, with fasting and weeping, and with mourning; and rend your hearts and not your garments."

God is Gracious

Joel could urge the people to repent and turn to God, because God was not only merciful, but God desired to serve this people so that never again would they be put to shame. (2:27) Furthermore, as God would deal out of grace with this wayward people, God desired to deal with them in a new and helpful manner in pouring out God's Spirit upon them. What had been shared with the people through called prophets would be shared in a new way. "Your sons and daughters shall prophesy, your old men shall dream dreams, and your young men shall see visions." (2:28) Centuries later the vision of the prophet Joel is cited in the great Pentecostal sermon of the apostle Peter as being fulfilled. (Acts 2:15-21)

As the great prophets before him, Joel took great comfort in the fact that God did not only visit wrath upon Judah as had been evidenced in the plague of the locust and its aftermath. God also ruled over all the nations. As God would vindicate Judah for her faith, so God would also work vengeance upon "all the nations and bring them down to the valley of

Jehoshaphat'' where God would enter into judgment with them. (3:1, 2) Once more God would dwell in Zion, and everyone would know that God is a refuge for the people, ''a stronghold to the people of Israel.'' (3:16-21) The prophet had come on the scene at a time of great devastation to call the people to repentance and to offer them a living hope in the God who says, ''I, the Lord, am your God and there is none else.'' (2:27)

16. Malachi

THE CATECHIST

The prophet Malachi was wearied by the complaint in his day. We are not sure who Malachi was. His name, which means, "Messenger," may have been adapted from his own oracles. (2:7 and 3:1) Whether that was his actual name or not is not known. However, what constitutes the book of what we call Malachi is a consistent effort on the part of a prophetic figure to give answer to nagging questions of the people who moaned and groaned at the apparent indifference of God to the plight of his people.

Why?

The prophet Malachi lived sometime after the people of God had returned from the Babylonian Exile. This (500-450 B.C.) was supposed to be that glorious era of which previous prophets had spoken. This was to be the golden age in which the fortunes of Israel would be restored. The City of God was to be rebuilt and the people of God were to enjoy peace and prosperitiy that would give eloquent testimony to the rule of God. But that is not the way it was at all. The times were just plain lousy. The city had not been rebuilt. Not all the people had returned from Babylon. In fact, those who had found new fortunes in Babylon tended to remain there. The people of God were in total disarray and seemingly had no great promise for the future. No wonder that the people were embittered and mournful about their prospects under the rule of God! They could not help but ask if God were not holding out on them and they wanted to know, "WHY?"

What constitutes the book of Malachi is a studied effort to give satisfactory answers to the puzzled questions of the people. The prophet offered several explanations. The first explanation for the trouble the people experienced was that much of it was of their own doing. He suggested that if the people had done what they should have, things could have been much better. They could have applied themselves much more. They could have expected much greater blessings, if they had been more diligent in their worship, more pious in their piety, and the like. (1:6—2:9) That should be so obvious. God does reward goodness. Good stewardship is blessed.

Complications

However, the prophet did not keep it all that simple either. He saw life far more complicated than that. (1:2-5) He could also see that there were plenty of inequities in the world. He knew that other people appeared to be more blessed at times even though they were in no way faithful to Jahweh, the God of Israel. He realized that much of what happens in the world is inexplicable. He knew that there were times when the most irresponsible people are the ones who seem to get away with it. He had no explanation for that. However, he did know that finally God's will is done.

Malachi pointed to the fate of the Edomites who had recently experienced great set backs as a people. (1:2-4) The people in Edom had been on top of it when the people of God were languishing. However, now the tables were turned. The prophet almost appears to take some delight in this fact. However, he does so only that he could use the situation as an example of how God does work out his purpose in his own time and that none can mock God for long. From the little people to the big people who ride high for the moment he could say, "You cannot defy the will of God without paying the price."

In general, the prophet observes, people cannot give up on the notion that God simply is not fair. No matter how one may try to hold out ultimate hope for people, their personal problems seem so great a burden, that they keep on with their complaints that everyone else does evil in the sight of God and still he rewards them. The prophet says that God is sick and tired of hearing that. (2:17) And one day God will suddenly come to his temple. (3:1) His messenger will go before him to prepare the way for him. His messenger is to cleanse the temple for him in preparing the way. The Lord is pictured as a King who comes to his palace. Just as a large entourage of people prepare the way for the president of the United States or some foreign dignitary when they come to our cities, so someone had to prepare the way for the king. Everything had to be made ready. All obstacles had to be removed. Threats to his life had to be eliminated by getting rid of those who would endanger his coming. The way had to be made beautiful.

In order for people to receive the One who was coming, the Messianic figure, they would have to be prepared for his coming. Their hearts would have to be cleansed. Their minds had to be set right. They had to rid themselves of everything standing in the way of a clean and clear reception of God's mercy and goodness. (3:6-12)

Who Can Endure?

But the prophet raises the question, "But who can endure the day of his coming, and who can stand when he appears?" (3:2) To prepare and repent for the coming of the King is an awesome task. "For he is like a refiner's fire and like fuller's soap; he will sit as a refiner and purifier of silver, and he will purify the sons of Levi and refine them like gold and silver, till they present right offerings to the Lord." (3:2, 3) The question is, are they ready to give up all that stands in the way of God coming to them?

The prophet believed that when the people would properly prepare for the messianic age, then God would come. He believed that when the people cleaned up their act, God could come to them. The prophet also realized what a difficult thing this was for the people to do. (3:13, 14) However, the prophet recognized that the reason that this people was not consumed was because of the God of the Covenant who does not change. He believed that the people should be able to discern the grace and kindness of a longsuffering God. They could see that he spared them out of his goodness. The prophet says that will be the same as a man "who spares his son who serves him" and looks upon the son as a "special possession." That, he says, will be the marked distinction between "the righteous and the wicked." (3:17, 18) The righteous are the ones who recognize that God wants to behave toward them as a father. Whatever they give up by way of repentance is not much. They gain everything. They gain the good pleasure, good will and love of God.

Repentant people have given up the false hope that they can make it on their own. They have lost no dignity. God is the one who confers dignity upon them by his love and his claim of them as his children. Because they gain so much in this exchange of their self-conceived worth and their self-styled dignity for the gift of God's acceptance. They do not have to be anxious about themselves. They do not have to prove themselves. Because they are acceptable to God, they are able to love themselves and to endure the judgments of the world. If they pass the fire of God's judgment then certainly the judgment of the world is nothing by comparison. The prophet could announce God's promise, "But for you who fear my name the sun of righteousness shall rise with healing in its wings. You shall go forth leaping like calves from the stall and you shall tread down the wicked for they will be ashes under the souls of your feet." (4:2, 3) The Christian community identified the Lord Jesus as the Son of Righteousness, who came to fulfill the promise, and Jesus himself identified the messenger (3:1) as John the Baptizer. (Matthew 11:10)

17. Daniel

THE HEROIC PROPHET

For centuries the Mediterranean world had been fascinated with Greek culture. However, it was Alexander the Great who extended the influence of Greek thought throughout the world of his day. As Alexander stretched the boundaries of his empire from the Nile all the way to the far reaches of India, he also made the process of hellenization indelible upon the world. His brief and dazzling career of spectacular conquests ended in 323 B.C. when he died at the age of thirty-three from a fever in India. Alexander had changed the world politically and culturally. Greek became the language of the world, and the process of hellenization continued long after Alexander.

Alexander's empire was divided and the Seleucid control of Palestine fell to Antiochus the Great, who lost control of Palestine and then regained it. Control of Palestine remained in the hands of the Greeks, and a Greek gymnasium was built in Jerusalem. Antiochus IV Epiphanes sold the priesthood. The temple was desecrated, and the religious practices of the Jews were violated. The situation in Jerusalem became critical. Some of the people had been willing to be assimilated into the Greek culture. Others became passive. Some resisted and created an uprising, the Maccabean revolt about 165 B.C. It was probably at this time that the Book of Daniel was written as an inspiration for people to stand firm in the Hebrew faith and resist hellenization.

Temptation 1 — Fasting

The Book of Daniel is listed among the prophets in our Bible. In the Hebrew Bible it is not arranged with the prophets,

87

but with the "Writings," the Hagiographa. The book which is strongly apocalyptic, was written both in Aramaic (2:4b—7:28) and Hebrew. (1:1—2:4a; 8:1—12:13). The book is composed of a collection of six stories about Daniel and his friends and a collection of visions which came to Daniel. The Hero Daniel is cited by the prophet Ezekiel as a legendary figure of strength (14:14) and wisdom. (28:3)

The first story about Daniel (Chapter 1) reports that when Nebuchadnezzar deported Hebrew captives to Babylon, some were selected for court service. At the court Daniel and his friends refused to eat from the King's table since this would have violated Hebrew dietary laws. Because of their refusal they were restricted to vegetables and water. However they thrived on this meager diet and proved to be healthier than others. God blessed their faithfulness with the gift of wisdom and they were proven to be of top drawer quality at the court. The implication of the story is very plain. One does not have to conform to the culture and social pressures of alien forces to gain recognition. Obedience to the commandments and ordinances of God is blessed by God and produces superior results.

Temptation 2 — Worship

The second temptation story is the account of the Three Confessors in the Fiery Furnace. (Chapter 3) The story of Shadrach, Meshach, and Abednego is so well rehearsed in legend and song that it hardly bears repeating. However, what is important to understand is that the intention of the story is to demonstrate that to suffer martyrdom for the sake of the faith is preferable to the denial of the faith. Nebuchadnezzar, according to the story, attempted to create a universal religion by having a huge image fashioned which all the people could worship. The ceremony of dedication was to be attended by representatives of the many people whom Babylonians had conquered. When the three Hebrew representatives failed to conform to the order to bow down and worship the golden image, they were hailed before the king.

The defense of the three faithful ones was that they believed their God could deliver them from the flames of the fiery furnace, but they were willing to suffer the consequences rather than "serve your gods or worship the golden image which you have set up." (3:18) The outcome was that the three men were attended by an angel in the furnace that had been heated up to a higher temperature because Nebuchadnezzar had been boiling at the confession of the three. The clothes of the three were not even singed by the fire. They were set free and the king declared that none should speak anything negative about the Hebrew God, and the three faithful Hebrews were promoted in the king's court. The teaching is plain. Those who do not conform to idolatrous worship will be blessed.

Temptation 3 — Prayer

A third temptation story is the story of Daniel in the Lion's Den. (Chapter 6) According to the story, after the Persians had destroyed the Babylonian Empire, Daniel had been elevated to the position of one of three presiding officers over some one hundred twenty provinces. When it was obvious that Daniel was the most proficient of the three, the king intended to appoint Daniel the whole kingdom. Daniel's colleagues tried to head that off by finding fault with him and realized that the only obvious flaw in the man and his work was the difference in their religious practice and worship. They plotted to have the king deliver an edict that no one could pray to any god or man except to the king.

The trap was set, and of course, Daniel was its victim because he continued to pray as always. Consequently, he was thrown into the lion's den only to have an anxious king greatly relieved when Daniel was spared the lion's mouth because of the presence of an angel of God. The king ordered the enemies of Daniel to be thrown to the lions and issued a degree that all honor the God of Daniel. The story was most appropriate for that time when Antiochus Epiphanes had forbidden the observance of the Sabbath, plundered and desecrated the temple, and for two years outlawed the practices of Judaism. Faithful Hebrews refused to conform and continued their religious rites and endured martyrdom.

The Dreams

In addition to the heroic and faithful stance that Daniel and his friends demonstrated in the face of severe temptation, Daniel also exhibited great sagacity in the interpretation of dreams. When King Nebuchadnezzer was troubled by dreams he could not understand, (Chapter 2) Chaldean magi were summoned to interpret the dreams but were stumped by them. Consequently, the lives of the wise men were threatened. Daniel was ordered to cooperate in the execution of the wise men. Daniel was shocked by the severity of the order and volunteered to interpret the dream. In a vision the answer was revealed to him that the king had been dreaming of the succession of five kingdoms that would all eventually perish followed by the establishment of the universal kingdom of God "which shall never be destroyed, nor shall its sovereignty be left to another people." (2:44) The story contrasts the ineptness of the wisest people of the earth compared to the wisdom God gives.

Nebuchadnezzer came to rely upon the wisest person in his court, Daniel, whom he called by the Babylonian name of Belteshazzar (2:26) to interpret another dream of a great tree. Daniel advised the king that the great tree was a symbol of this greatness that had to be cut down in order that he might through repentance acknowledge the power of the Most High. (Chapter 4) The king would also suffer some insanity for a time before he would be restored. Once more the lesson is clear. The greatest powers are helpless without God.

Daniel continued in the royal court of Babylon through the rule of several sovereigns. He interpreted the handwriting on the wall at a feast in which Belshazzar and his court defiled the previous vessels from the temple in Jerusalem with the debauchery and toasting of their idols. (Chapter 5) The handwriting was discernable enough. Babylon would fall and would be divided among the Medes and the Persians. The story is one more case history that sacrilege will not go unpunished.

The Visions

The second part of the Book of Daniel contains four visions which came to Daniel during his continuing career as the renowned seer of the royal court of Babylon.

The Book of Daniel has been fertile territory for those who like to manipulate its apocalyptic imagery and make it fit their personal predictions for the future. However, the book is most helpful when it is understood in its context as comfort, inspiration, and hope for the people suffering the tyranny of Antiochus Epiphanes. For the faithful it is a similar message of strength to face the trials and temptations of any age.

The book was a resource of consolation for the Hebrews facing one holocaust after another as well as for Christians who faced persecution because of the faith. Temptations and tests of the faith are more subtle where the faithful enjoy religious freedom. Yet the people who lived when the process of hellenization was at work and was the "in thing," must have faced the same stress and pressures as people today who are more concerned about identifying with the culture rather than the faith. The Book of Daniel brings the temptations into perspective and reminds us that cultures, like kingdoms, will pass. To the faithful like Daniel, however, the angel says, "Go your way to the end; and you shall rest, and shall stand in your allotted place at the end of the days." (12:13)

18. Jonah

THE RELUCTANT PROPHET

The Book of Jonah is completely different from all other prophetic books. The prophets are collections of their sermons, poems, hymns, psalms, oracles, parables and sayings. We have only scanty biographical or autobiographical details in these books. Jonah, however, is a story about a prophet. In this book we have scanty material that are sermons and teachings, but have considerable detail concerning a couple important events. The purpose of telling this story is very clear. The people of Judah, after the Exile, had become sadly disillusioned about their fathers and the reason for their loss of prestige in the world. They had vowed that this loss of identity would never occur again. They began to call themselves Jews from the name of their tribe. They developed schools or synagogues to teach carefully their tradition. They cut themselves off from other Semites or half-Semites like the Samaritans. They became extremely isolationistic and believed that salvation belonged only to the Jews.

Wicked Nineveh

In that context comes this book about a prophet whom God called to go to the city of Nineveh. To understand the importance of that we must realize that Nineveh was not a Jewish city. It was an Assyrian capital. As such it was representative not only of an alien people but also a people that had been hostile to the Jews. It represented power and wealth. It boasted worship of other gods than Jahweh, the God of Israel. In Jewish terms it would have to be regarded as a wicked city. That is how God sees it, too. He calls the prophet, "Arise, go to Nineveh, that great city, and cry against it for their wickedness has come up before me." (1:2) The call is too much for Jonah. He is intimidated. Either he thinks the city is too big, the city is too wicked, the city does not deserve a Word from God, or his life is in jeopardy. It may have been all of these things, or a combination of some of them, or just any one of them. He resists God's call and heads in the other direction. Instead of grabbing a boat to Nineveh, he pays for a fare on a ship he believes will take him "away from the presence of the Lord." He ships off for Tarshish instead of Nineveh. He ran from God. He thought he could duck the responsibility God laid on him.

Comes the Storm

What happened when Jonah tried that is well known. The boat he was riding got caught in a terrible storm. The captain did the best he could to fight the storm. They lighted the load of the ship. When that did nothing for them, the captain invited all his men to pray to their gods. And when all heads were to be on deck Jonah was sleeping in the hold of the ship. They woke him in a hurry and asked him to pray. Then the crew decided they should cast lots to see which party aboard ship was responsible for this disaster sent by the gods. The lot fell to Jonah, and he was asked to explain who he was and what he was doing. He told them. They asked what they should do with him. He replied that they should throw him overboard. They tried once more to row to shore, but to no avail. They then threw Jonah overboard. The storm ceased, and of course, the men were greatly impressed and made a sacrifice to God.

God appointed a great fish to swallow Jonah, and he was in the fish for three days and three nights. Jonah prayed in the fish's belly, and God heard his prayer. "The Lord spoke to the fish, and it vomited Jonah upon the dry land." (2:10) There was no way this prophet could run from the Lord and flee from his presence. The Psalmist says, "If I take the wings of the morning and dwell in the uttermost parts of the sea, even there thy hand shall hold me, and thy right hand shall hold me." (Psalm 139:9)

After the fish spat up Jonah on the dry ground "the word of the Lord came to Jonah the second time." (3:1) God did not give up on his purpose to save the city of Nineveh. He calls Jonah to go to that great city and proclaim His word to it. Jonah is to be God's herald. Regardless of how Jonah feels about the situation God wants him to do this work for him.

Comes the Dawn

Jonah finally got the message. Reluctantly he went to Nineveh, and he preached. The author says it was a big city, "three days' journey in breadth." A day's journey would be twenty miles. That means this city would be sixty miles across. That is larger than most metropolitan areas today. That must have taken in the whole territory, counties and suburbs around Nineveh. What the author undoubtedly wants to suggest is that this was a big city. When he says that Jonah went a day's journey into the city, he means that he went to the heart of the city. That is where he unloaded this message from God. "Yet forty days, and Nineveh shall be overthrown." He preached this dire threat from God. The city is going to be destroyed because it is so wicked.

They Believed

Now, wonder of wonders! The whole city "believed God." They believed that Jonah was a prophet sent from God. They believed this call to repentance. The King of Nineveh himself went into mourning and proclaimed a fast for all the people including all the animals. He calls on all the people to forsake their evil ways in the hope that God would repent, change his mind and be merciful to the people. The people do just what the king requested. And "when God saw what they did . . . God repented of the evil which he said he would do to them." (3:10) God was gracious toward them and saved them. Now who should be the most happy about all this? Jonah, of course. But he is not. He becomes angry that God spares the city. He said he had expected God to be gracious toward him when he ran away. Why should he have come here to be disgraced by this God who now spares this awful wicked city?

Jonah wanted only God's grace for himself but he wanted it for no one else. He was a legalist of the worst sort. He wanted to be a hellfire and brimstone preacher and wanted to prove the wrath of God to everyone. He could believe in a God who miraculously spares him by permitting a fish to swallow him and vomit him on the shore, but he could not believe in a God who would forgive a wicked but repentant city. The next day God gives him another lesson in his grace and love. Jonah sleeps under a gourd that gives him shade. But God permits a worm to eat up the gourd and it withers away. Once more Jonah is angry. God asks him why he should pity a plant for which he did not labor or work. So God asks, "And should I not pity Nineveh, that great city, in which there are more than a hundred and twenty thousand persons who do not know their right hand from their left, and also much cattle?" (4:11)

The Sign of Jonah

The story ends with that question. There is no answer given as to how Jonah felt after that or what he did. You can guess why. The people who first heard this story or read the book and all who have heard it since are to give the answer. There is no historical evidence that the city of Nineveh ever had this mass conversion to the faith of Jahweh. But the story makes its point. God's grace is universal. It is for all nations, all peoples, people of all ages, all colors, or classes. They are the objects of God's love. God proved that when his own Son came to fulfill the sign of Jonah.

Jesus said, "As Jonah was three days and three nights in the belly of the whale, so will the Son of Man be three days and three nights in the heart of the earth. The men of Nineveh

96

will arise at the judgment with this generation and condemn it; for they repented at the preaching of Jonah, and behold something greater than Jonah is here.'' (Matthew 12:39-41) Jesus is the One greater than Jonah who came as the sign of God's grace for us in His death and resurrection. In him, in the word about him, the Gospel of God's love, we are not only saved and can repent, but we can become his sons and daughters sent to proclaim the good news of his love.